TEACH YOUR CHILD
TO READ IN *60* DAYS

TEACH YOUR CHILD TO READ IN *60* DAYS

by Sidney Ledson

W·W·NORTON & COMPANY·INC·

NEW YORK

Library of Congress Cataloging in Publication Data

Ledson, Sidney.
    Teach your child to read in 60 days.

    Includes bibliographical references.
    1. Reading (Preschool)   2. Domestic education.
I. Title.
LB1140.5.R4142   372.4'1   75–5838
ISBN 0–393–08709–3

PRINTED IN THE UNITED STATES OF AMERICA
1 2 3 4 5 6 7 8 9 0

Contents

Acknowledgments

My warm thanks to Rachel Ladouceur; Margaret Hill, head of the Education Clinic, Ottawa Board of Education; Margaret Main and her associates at the Ottawa Public Library; Ann Cleery, librarian, U.S. Embassy, Ottawa; officers of the Reading Reform Foundation; and to those who helped at the beginning when it was very important: Heather Hand, Hilda MacLean, and Cynthia Ross.

Special thanks to Daphne Overhill for sagacious editorial surgery, the worth of which will be remembered long after the pain is forgotten.

Finally, lasting thanks to the many teacher-assistants, aged eight to sixteen, who have helped in the children's education—especially: Lisa and Cathy Stone, Shelagh Burke, Karrin, Sandy, and Marg Rita Wright, Lana Toole, Diane Gervais, Vivian Bibby, Katherine Neuspiel, Karen Davidson, and Debbie Brown.

PART 1

There is only one road to progress, in education as in other human affairs, and that is: Science wielded by love. Without science, love is powerless; without love, science is destructive.
—Bertrand Russell, *On Education*

CHAPTER 1

Blowing Out Candles
for Fun and Profit

Six large pieces of colored cardboard are tacked to the ceiling in my daughters' bedroom. Three of the cards display the letters **a**, **b**, and **c** printed 10 inches high, in strokes 1 inch thick, big enough to ensure easy recognition as the girls lie in their cribs. The other three cards present the first three words the children learned to read—**cab**, **scab**, and **bac** (with the **k** purposely left off).

The cards have been displayed there for fourteen months, and are beginning to fade and curl. They serve no purpose now but to amuse visitors. I should take them down. But, raising two infants single-handedly, earning a living, and writing this book keep me busy enough nights, week ends, and holidays without my looking around for more chores. The cards are safe up there for a while.

Since I tacked the cards up, the children have read three hundred books, some of them more than once, of course— some as many as ten times. So, the children have read, in bulk, the equivalent of about five hundred books ranging in difficulty from their first, *The Lion and the Deer* (eighty-four-word vocabulary), to those suitable for third-grade pupils (aged eight and nine).

WHEN IS A CHILD REALLY READING?

We began our reading adventure fourteen months ago, on August 27, 1972—Eve was three years, eleven months old, Jean was two years, nine months—and at the end of sixty days the girls had mastered what seemed to be the essentials of reading. They were then able to read 186 words,[1] singly or in any sentence that could be formed with the words, proved by a simple device that created an endless variety of sentences. The children could read in upper- or lower-case letters, and in 10-point type (normal typewriter size).

In addition, the children were able to pronounce most other words spelled in a simple, phonically regular way. Even if the girls had not seen nor heard the word before—as in the case of **fig, swell, plenty, fan, problem**—one or the other child was able to sound each correctly without help.

The children didn't acquire this skill in sixty days by plan, for there was no plan; it simply took us that long by the methods I happened to hit on. Was ours a fair demonstration of true reading ability? You may want to suspend judgment until you learn what passes for reading in some schools. In my own mind, I felt we had achieved a point of "lift-off" at the end of those sixty days.[2] After that, I had only to enlarge the children's reading and speaking vocabularies.

AN AMATEUR AND AN APPRENTICE

Do you think my daughters were exceptionally clever? I'd like to think so, but the women who look after them each day

1. Listed on page 148.
2. Later, I learned that our accomplishments met the standards set by Dolores Durkin in a study of California school children. Dr. Durkin's goal in that research project was to learn how preschool reading ability affects children's later academic ability. Children were considered "readers" if they could read aloud any eighteen words in a special list of thirty-seven. At the end of sixty days, my daughters were reading twenty-one of these words, and their decoding skill was sufficiently good that, had they been shown the list (which I didn't have at that time), the girls would probably have been able to read three or four words more. One small distinction—the words in the test list were to be read in 18-point type, whereas Eve and Jean were already reading at almost half that size.

at their nursery [3] are of the opinion, stated cautiously but candidly, that neither child is unusually bright.

If, as it seems, the girls have just average intelligence, you might suppose I was a highly qualified teacher. This isn't the case. First, I was not and am not certified to teach an academic subject to anyone, whether child or adult. Second, I had never worked with children before and, frankly, I'm still not attracted to the job. I'm simply a writer interested in effective educational methods. I taught my daughters to read only because I believed the skill shouldn't be delayed any longer and because there was no one else to teach them.

Another reason for our reading program was to let the children enjoy stories at bedtime; [4] it's a nice part of childhood. Though I wished them this pleasure, I was seldom able to provide it, for, by the time the children were fed, washed, and in bed, I was usually too tired or in too poor a mood to read fairy tales. The next best thing, therefore, was to teach the girls to read their own bedtime stories.

Viewing the reading lessons thus—as a temporary extra chore that would eventually richen the children's lives—I began our program. However, when an opportunity arose three months later to let someone else handle the teaching, I quickly took advantage of it. And so it was a neighbor, Lynn Rivett, who helped the children to read their first fifty books.

You may think that Lynn Rivett was a first-rate teacher. Well, no, not really. Lynn had even less teaching experience than I. She merely relied on a loose set of instructions I gave her. Mind you, Lynn did an excellent job of teaching the children—there's no doubt about it—especially when you consider she was only thirteen years old.

Now, it seems to me that if a writer and a thirteen year old can raise two mentally unspectacular infants up to third-grade reading level quickly, then an average parent should be able to do as much by using the same techniques. This book describes our program, explains why the instruction

---

3. Some people distinguish between a nursery and a day-care center; however, for brevity, the term *nursery* will be used throughout the book.

4. There are a number of stories children should *not* be exposed to at bedtime, or at any other time for that matter. These are discussed on page 193.

took the curious form it did, and tells how you can apply these techniques to your own child's education.

There is good reason to suspect that you may even surpass our achievements, for we were handicapped in three ways. First, there *wasn't* any sixty-day reading program when we started—it hadn't been created yet. The program *couldn't* be devised in advance because I knew nothing of reading instruction. I had never taught children to read so I had no idea what the problems were, much less how to solve them. Only as we moved ahead, slowly and with repeated failure, did it become apparent which direction we should take. In a sense, we were building a road while driving along it. Therefore, some of the sixty days indicated by the title of this book were actually wasted in trying methods that were eventually abandoned.

A second handicap was the lack of time available for our program. The reading sessions were restricted to periods before 8:30 in the morning, after 5:30 at night and to week ends. Lack of space imposed its own special restrictions too. My being in debt from a business failure demands that we live in a one-bedroom apartment. The girls have the bedroom; I have the main room for living quarters and studio (at the moment my income is derived from free-lance artwork).[5]

The final and most trying handicap was the teaching of two children at once. You might think that each child's learning had reinforced the other's by double exposure to the material. Unfortunately, this didn't happen. Instead of paying attention to each other's attempts to read, the children ignored one another completely and presented an imaginative program of distractions. So, my usual task was to coach one child and fire her enthusiasm, while trying to restrain or ignore the gymnastic demonstrations of the other.

Under other circumstances, of course, the presence of a second child might *not* be a hindrance and might even be an asset. In any case, the sixty-day reading program can be used for one or two children—or even three or four, depending on the conditions in the home. However, the more children tak-

---

5. I have two careers—one as an artist, the other as a writer.

ing part, the longer each child will have to wait his turn, and this might lower enthusiasm.

WATCHING THE CALENDAR AND HOPING

My repeated mention of time and speed of learning may give the impression that speed alone, perhaps the setting of a quick-reading record, was the goal of our program. However, my concern for speed was similar to that of a swimmer pursued by alligators—he may reach shore in record time, but he wasn't really too concerned about setting a record.

My own personal "alligators" took the form of limited patience for working with children, and business matters that neither favored nor permitted a long reading program. Our program *had* to be brief or risk abandonment. The sooner the children learned to read, the sooner I could get on with other matters that interested me more. I had no idea how long the reading chore would take, or what methods would be used, but I was convinced that there were undiscovered ways to hasten the business. And, as it turned out, there were.

How did we accomplish so much so quickly? By playing a variety of games; and so the program was not work for the children, but play. Several devices were used to keep enthusiasm high. In fact, the girls sometimes clamored to play the games before they were out of bed in the morning. And, of course, every game increased their knowledge of reading. One particularly efficient game taught the children new words at the speed of six words in six minutes.

WHAT'S HAPPENING IN SCHOOLS THESE DAYS?

Having heard now how quickly children can be taught to read, you may wonder, as I did, why schools find it so difficult to teach children to read in two, three, and even four or more years despite a wealth of materials and highly trained staffs. One might suspect that teaching a class of forty children is much more difficult than teaching just two, but this would ignore the fact that school reading programs are specially designed to capitalize on the presence of many. So,

puzzled by the apparent poor performance of schools, I went
to my favorite university, the public library, and began taking
out every book available on school reading instruction.

I am no longer puzzled by the inefficiency of schools. What
I have discovered will interest you, astonish you, and perhaps even anger you. Assuming you are or plan to be the
parent of a child, the methods used in schools will eventually
concern you. In fact, school methods will be an important
point for you to ponder when deciding whether or not to
teach your child reading *before* he goes to school.

HOW LEARNING IS ACCELERATED

Learning is made easy or difficult solely by the way material is presented to the learner. Few subjects are really difficult in themselves. Most subjects we consider difficult—
nuclear physics, for example—are not "difficult" but merely
"advanced," and when we know all the bits of information
that lead up to the study of an advanced subject, it becomes
easy.

Good presentation of material hastens learning. And when
material is presented in a manner that makes forgetting difficult, learning becomes quicker still. "Guaranteed remembrance" is part and parcel of good teaching. But how can
remembrance be secured? In several ways. Here's one
method.

Suppose you were studying astronomy. The teacher might
begin with a discussion of the solar system, and explain, by
use of film slides and perhaps an orrery (a mechanical device
that simulates the movement of the nine planets around the
sun), how the system operates. You would learn the order of
the planets, beginning with the one nearest the sun: Mer-
cury, Venus, Earth, Mars, Jupiter, Saturn, Uranus, Neptune,
Pluto.

Now, if at any future time you wanted to discuss the solar
system, it would be useful if you could remember this order.
How long would you need to commit the order to memory?
Most people would probably need about half an hour plus
occasional reviews of the material for a week or so. However,

my friend Ray Stone has reduced the time needed for the job to two minutes. Simply commit his following nonsense sentence to memory: "Many very early men just sat under new potatoes." You'll find that each word in this sentence bears just enough resemblance to the name of the planet it represents to let you recall that planet's name easily. Here are the words of the sentence arranged for easier comparison:

many	very	early	men	just
Mercury	Venus	Earth	Mars	Jupiter

sat	under	new	potatoes
Saturn	Uranus	Neptune	Pluto

Trick? Of course; but it works. Would we be able to remember how many days there were in each month if we hadn't a rhyme to help us? And how would we remember which months oysters were firmest and tastiest if we didn't know that the last letter of oyster should be found in the names of those months?

Naturally, all learning problems can't be solved by the use of limericks, jingles, and rhymes, but the inventive skill that originated these memory aids could as easily find other novel, imaginative ways to make learning enjoyable and remembering easy if directed to that task. Imaginative methods simplify both the teacher's job and the pupil's. Sometimes just a single idea can mean the difference between success and failure of a project or between slow learning and quick, as in the following case.

HOW TO MASTER A WIND INSTRUMENT IN FIFTEEN MINUTES

Do you like puzzles? Here's a puzzle. My younger daughter, Jean,[6] still hadn't learned to blow her nose at age three. Despite coaching, she continued to sniff air *into* her nostrils instead of blowing out. Worse, she was always catching

---

6. An easy way to distinguish my elder daughter from her sister is to remember that the name of the first-born, Eve, is the same as the Biblical first woman.

colds, and the inability to clear her nose increased her discomfort. Someone told me about a child who hadn't learned
to blow his nose until the age of eight. The thought of a five-
year wait for Jean to discover the nose-blowing trick was
stunning. But how on earth do you teach a child to blow her
nose? (Dr. Spock missed this one.)

Don't feel bad if you can't immediately think of a solution.
It took me two weeks to find one. There are probably better
ways to solve the problem, but here is how I finally went
about it.

I held a lighted candle ahead of and below Jean's nose,
told her to take a deep breath, close her mouth tightly, and
hold her breath for a couple of seconds. When she breathed
out—through her nose—she did so, of course, with enough
force to disturb the candle's flame. This delighted her. By
having Jean repeat the exercise and breathe out a little more
quickly, she saw how the flame could be upset even more;
but when she saw the flame could actually be blown out in
this way, the youngster became a virtual nose pump. Twenty
burnt matches later, the problem of nose blowing was far
behind us.

MAKING MUSCLES PULL THEIR WEIGHT

Teaching a child to read is a fairly simple task compared
with teaching him to talk. To read, a child need merely memorize various letter-sound relationships plus a few irregularities—a goal lying well within his mental ability, and, as we
will see later, well within his visual ability.

In learning to talk, however, a child must learn to control a
whole set of muscles in new ways, and it is physically impossible for us to help him gain this control. We can't pull this or
that muscle taut for him, or relax some other unneeded muscle. The only way we can help the struggling child speak is
to encourage and reward him with praise whenever his fal-
tering efforts approximate the desired performance. When a
baby learns to say "Ma-ma" and "Da-da," he has no idea at
first what these sounds mean; but he soon learns that the
sounds cause two big people—people very important to
him—to become pleasantly excited.

Some muscular skills are simple for children to learn; others are difficult. For example, walking is easy; whistling is not. And to confound any tidy generalization on the subject, there are at least two muscular skills children can master easily if they're in the right mood—the control of urination and defecation. Most children "decide" to stop messing their pants by the age of three. However, the December 4, 1972, issue of *Newsweek* tells how two psychologists have helped children opt for tidy pants at even earlier ages.

THE POTTY PSYCHOLOGISTS

Nathan H. Azrin and Richard M. Foxx of the Illinois State Hospital at Anna, have devised a program to toilet train two year olds in about four hours. When the wind is favorable and God is in His heaven, the psychologists can reduce this time to ninety minutes.

The child is given all the pop he can drink. The researchers check his pants every few minutes and, if dry, the child is rewarded with praise, hugging, and potato chips. The youngster is introduced to a Thirsty Baby doll and told to give the doll a big drink of water. When the doll "pees," the specially designed potty plays the tune "Mary Had a Little Lamb." The child is then urged to reward the doll with a potato chip. The idea here is that the infant learns more about the reward by being the one who delivers it. The child is further conditioned by a series of questions.

"Does Santa wet his pants?"

"No."

"Do policemen pee-pee in their pants?"

"No."

If a child inadvertently wets his pants during the exercise, the rewards are withheld and he is simply told to change his pants. When dry, the child is praised, hugged, and given potato chips. What child could hold out for long against this sort of instruction? [7]

What has all this to do with teaching children to read? A lot. The techniques used by researchers Azrin and Foxx are

7. This method is now fully described in the book Nathan H. Azrin and Richard M. Foxx's *Toilet Training in Less than a Day* (New York, 1974).

the same ones that make the sixty-day program work—the dressing up of ideas by showmanship, and the selling of them by salesmanship. Motivation is strengthened by enthusiastic praise and material reward. In addition, the reading program employs games to generate fun and induce frequent repetition of the material to be learned.

But, you may ask, must a reading program for infants be turned into such a production? No, not at all. Only if you want them to master the reading skill quickly and easily. Throughout history, infants of two, three, and four years have learned to read without games or other aids. But in most cases, their parents had plenty of time to devote to instruction or they had plenty of money to pay tutors.

Children can be taught to read by several methods and they will be content with any of these so long as the teacher demonstrates patience and provides inducements. Youngsters aren't too concerned about the speed of a reading method because they're in no hurry. They have all the time in the world. But have you?

The sixty-day program will have particular appeal for parents who want their children to read early but who, because of their own personal alligators, can't tolerate a long reading program.

CHAPTER 2

Top Marks to the Pickled-brained Genius

You have heard of political wars, racial wars, and religious wars. I'd like to tell you now about an educational war, one that has been raging for the past seventy-five years, one which, at this moment, shows no sign of stopping. This particular war involves children, the age they should be taught to read, and the method by which they should be taught. Like all wars, this one has its casualties. Here, they appear as handicapped readers and lame spellers. Because *your* child could be among those afflicted, you will be interested in knowing some of the strong beliefs at issue and some of the stout defenders of those beliefs.

When your child enters first grade, he will receive reading instruction. The method used to teach him can have a profound effect on whether he becomes a proficient, adventurous reader or a timid, halting, unenthusiastic one. You have a right to know about the past performance of any method a teacher might employ in teaching your child to read. You have a right to know what relationship is likely to be formed between your child and the printed word. Let's begin by examining some beliefs that have shaped the present philosophy and performance of our school system.

AT WHAT AGE SHOULD CHILDREN BE TAUGHT TO READ?

Most North American children begin learning to read at age six and a half, and North American teachers think this is just about the right age for them to do so. (In England, children begin to read at age five, and English teachers, of course, think *that* is just about the right age.) However, the reason six and a half became the favored age for beginning reading in North America and the reason our entire school system is tightly locked to it are *not* generally known.

Age six and a half has become, and continues to be, the most popular age for reading commencement in North America mainly because of conclusions reached by Mabel Morphett and Carleton Washburne in their 1931 study of Winnetka, Illinois, school children. Their forty-two-year-old report remains to this day the most powerful single force working against any change of thought. We will look more closely at the findings of this research team later.

Other educators have favored different starting ages. For example, in 1898, John Dewey, philosopher and educationalist, stated that the human sense organs and nervous system in general were not adapted to such confining work as reading and writing before the age of eight. Moreover, Dewey was convinced that reading instruction before this age could enfeeble a child's mind.

THERE HAVE BEEN EXCEPTIONS

Even allowing for some frighteningly complex phonetic alphabets in use at that time,[1] Dewey's blanket condemnation of reading before age eight through fear of mental injury had no basis. Historically, early reading ability, far from promoting mental feebleness, appears to promote high intelligence and sometimes genius.

---

1. Most phonetic alphabets were similar to those now used in dictionaries to indicate word-pronunciation. One early phonetic alphabet for reading instruction employed 92 symbols for the sounds of the lower-case letters and another 92 for the upper-case letters—a total of 184 characters!

In her book, *A Genetic Study of Genius,* volume 2 (Stanford, Calif., 1959), Dr. Catherine Cox reports that Jeremy Bentham (1748–1832), the English jurist and philosopher, had learned the alphabet before he could talk.[2] When Bentham was three, his father introduced a Latin grammar and other books into his son's education. Young Bentham read Rapine's *History of England* that same year.

Thomas Macaulay (1800–1859), English historian and statesman, read incessantly at age three—"telling interminable stories from his reading or from his imagination." Blaise Pascal (1623–1662), French mathematician and inventor, was another early reader. When Blaise was three, his father devoted his full time to teaching the boy and other members of the family. Charles Darwin's cousin, Sir Francis Galton (1822–1911), an anthropologist who, among other things, systematized fingerprinting methods for crime detection, knew all the capital letters when he was twelve months old, all the upper- and lower-case letters at eighteen months, and had read his first book at two and a half years.

Dr. Cox assigns a posthumous IQ rating of 180 each to Bentham, Pascal, and Macaulay. Estimating an IQ after the subject has died is much more complicated than adding up his score on an IQ test sheet. Points are assigned for such things as the person's earliest period of instruction, the nature of his earliest learning, his earliest productions, his first reading, his first mathematical calculations, his tendency to discriminate and generalize, and his other characteristically precocious activities.

ENTER JOHN STUART MILL, MENTAL COLOSSUS

Dr. Cox's book, a veritable "who's who" of genius, is also, significantly enough, a "who's who" of early readers. Now, if Bentham, Pascal, and Macaulay, with their IQs of 180, make the rest of us look mentally unspectacular, then the superstar of her book, John Stuart Mill, makes us look mentally re-

2. Dr. Cox doesn't mention how this feat was proved. We might assume that although young Jeremy couldn't speak words, he could sound the letters when shown them.

tarded, because Dr. Cox assigns Mill the staggering IQ of 190 to 200! By this measure, Mill must have approached the upper limit of human intellectual reach.

Was John Stuart Mill an early reader? You bet.

His father gave the boy an education without precedent. In his autobiography, John Stuart Mill has this to say of it: "I have no remembrance of the time when I began to learn Greek, I have been told that it was when I was three years old. My earliest recollection on the subject, is that of committing to memory what my father termed vocables, being lists of common Greek words with their signification in English, which he wrote out for me on cards."

But, for the most striking feature of Mill's education, we have to read between the lines. At age three, young Mill was able to tell the meaning of Greek words printed on cards by reading the English words that accompanied them. Fine, but when did he learn to read English? Though he mentions learning to read Greek at three and Latin at eight, nowhere in his detailed autobiography does he say when he learned to read English. But if he was employing his English-reading skill to learn Greek, he must have been taught to read English before the age of three—so early, in fact, that he had forgotten the process of instruction!

When Mill was of an age when most children read *The Three Little Pigs,* here is what he had read: "a number of Greek prose authors, among whom I remember the whole of Herodotus, and of Xenophon's Cyropaedia and Memorials of Socrates; some of the lives of the philosophers by Diogenes Laertius; part of Lucian, and Isocrates ad Demonicum and Ad Nicoclem. I also read, in 1813 [he was then 7], the first six dialogues—in the common arrangement—of Plato, from the Euthyphron to the Theoctetus inclusive: which last dialogue, I venture to think, would have been better omitted, as it was totally impossible I should understand it."

Perhaps Mill, Macaulay, Bentham, Galton, and Pascal were reading at an early age *because* they were bright. But if this were so, we should expect *all* brilliant children to read early and read well. Unfortunately they don't. In a study of seventy-seven children having IQs between 120 and 200, twenty-five were found to be reading at a level that wasn't even high enough for their *actual* age, let alone their mental age! [3]

Children read early and well if they are taught early and well, regardless of whether they are brilliant or not. Furthermore, evidence seems to suggest that if other factors in a child's life have not already secured his or her mental brilliance, then early reading skill can do so. As we will see later, the process of learning to read has a profound influence on the entire functioning of the brain.

EARLY READING RESEARCHED

In his monumental work, *A Genetic Study of Genius*, volume 1 (Stanford, Calif., 1959), Lewis Terman reveals that of 552 gifted children he studied, half had learned to read before they started school. Ruth Strang found the same proportion of preschool readers in a group of fifty-four junior-high-school students whose IQs were 120 or higher.[4] And what effect has preschool reading ability on school performance? Dolores Durkin recorded that fifteen out of forty-nine preschool readers were double promoted and went through primary school in six years instead of eight.[5]

Should we really be surprised at the apparent link between mental brilliance and early reading ability? Consider, in learning to read a child must master a complicated system of sound symbols and must learn to decode a ⅛-inch printed sound track in the form of twenty-six recurring marks. And to make the task more difficult, some of the marks or groups of marks represent more than one sound. Consider, too, the visual acuity a child must develop to detect tiny differences, as exists between the letters *c* and *e*.

3. M. L. Kellmer Pringle, *Able Misfits* (London, 1970).
4. "Reading Development of Gifted Children," *Elementary English* (January, 1954), 35–40.
5. Dolores Durkin, *Children Who Read Early* (New York, 1966).

THE NUMBERS GAME

Now to return to John Dewey. We would have to ignore the many distinguished leaders and scholars throughout history who learned to read in infancy if we were to subscribe to Dewey's curious recommendation for a postponement of reading instruction until age eight. Another voice in harmony with Dewey's at the turn of the century was G. T. W. Patrick, who pleaded for an even later commencement of reading because, as Patrick asserted, "the child's mind, before ten, has not ripened sufficiently for tasks like reading and writing." [6]

The oldest age suggested for learning to read is, apparently, fifteen, and it was advanced almost as a literary shrug by the educational pioneer, Jean Jacques Rousseau (1712–1778). In *Emile* (a work describing the ideal education of an imaginary child) Rousseau tells us, "Emile, at the age of twelve, will scarcely know what a book is. . . . What we are in no hurry to get is usually obtained with speed and certainty. I am pretty sure Emile will learn to read and write before he is ten, just because I care very little whether he can do so before he is fifteen. . . ."

Rousseau's world was much different from our own. People of that time were not surrounded by print. Reading was mainly a pastime, to be indulged or not in one's leisure moments. But in our modern urban society, the ability to read is almost as valuable as the ability to hear or smell. Patterns of personal conduct, inclinations—even potentialities—are well established before a child reaches fifteen, and if reading has not contributed to the formation of those characteristics, then reading will never be important to that person.

BACKERS OF EARLY READING

Some authorities favor reading instruction before six and a half. In England, Mr. Fred J. Schonell, whose textbooks on reading instruction are widely used, believes that six is just

6. G. T. W. Patrick, "Should Children under Ten Learn to Read and Write?," *Popular Science Monthly* (February, 1899), 382–392.

about right for reading, even though, ironically, English school children begin reading at five. Some schools admit children before their fifth birthday as "rising fives." A government publication says, "Indeed, in some areas where buildings and teachers are available, children start school even earlier. In January 1971 there were about 220,000 children under five in infant classes (mostly attending full-time but some 4,000 part-time); and about 100,000 more (45,000 full-time and 55,000 part-time) in some 500 separate nursery schools and 2,000 nursery classes in primary schools." [7]

From this report, we see that age four is becoming a common one for English children to begin reading.

On this side of the Atlantic, Dr. Arthur I. Gates urged, in 1937, reading commencement at age five. In fact, seventeen years later (1954) when Dr. Gates was a professor emeritus at the Institute of Language Arts, Teacher's College, Columbia University, he then advocated an even earlier age for beginning reading—age four.

Twenty years later, Dr. Gates's recommendations still go unheeded despite the findings of a study conducted in Denver between 1960 and 1966. About 4,000 kindergarten pupils received reading instruction, and an annual appraisal of the children's reading ability throughout their first five grades of school proved that children as young as four and a half could, and did, profit from reading instruction.

ENGLAND CONTINUES TO SET THE PACE

The voice of American researchers seems to be heard only in England, for there the teaching of reading will soon be started even earlier. *Education: A Framework for Expansion*, describes changes to be introduced over the next ten years. Subsection 13 declares, "The Government have decided to launch a new policy for the education of children under five. This will be the first systematic step since 1870, when education was made compulsory at the age of five, to offer an earlier start in education." The report then reveals a plan to pro-

7. *Education: A Framework for Expansion* (London, 1972), pp. 4–5.

vide education for all three and four year olds whose parents
wish to participate.

When I read this, my first thought was that the planners
probably intended to start the three year olds stringing beads
and pasting colored paper. But the British High Commission
assured me that early reading is to be a basic goal of the program, and that some nursery schools are, *already* teaching
three year olds to read.

English school children have traditionally learned to read a
year earlier than North American children. And, thanks to enterprising day nurseries, English children are more commonly reading *two* years before their North American counterparts. But now, because of an enlightened Ministry of
Education, English children will soon be reading *three* years
ahead of children in the United States and Canada.[8]

TEACHING BABIES TO READ

But, though English educators are actually putting theories
into practice by re-establishing the instruction of three year

8. Curiously enough, by exercising this "advanced" thinking, the Ministry
will merely be re-establishing an education practice of a hundred fifty years
ago. In the 1820s children as young as three received formal instruction in
schools managed by the London Infant School Society. One of the philan-
thropists responsible for the founding of these schools, Lord Henry
Brougham, summed up the philosophy of his group thus: "Schools . . . are
only open to children too far advanced in years. Whoever knows the habits
of children at an earlier age than six or seven—the age which they generally
attend the infant schools— . . . is well aware of their capacity to receive instruction long before the age of six . . . the truth is that he (the child) can
and does learn a great deal more before that age than all he ever learns or
can learn in all his life after." (House of Lords, 1835.)

Popular acceptance of this belief attracted more youngsters to the infant
schools and encouraged an even earlier commencement of learning. By
1871, 287,544 children below age five were being taught, 18,755 of whom
were under *three* (Board of Education Statistics, 1908–9, p. 18). And because
the teachings of Friedrich Froebel, the originator of kindergartens, had not
yet reached England, two-year-old school children were taught numbers and
letters in the same manner as older children. But educators gradually realized in the ensuing years that the elementary-school environment and its
disciplines was not suitable for babies. Consequently, the 1902 Education
Act virtually guaranteed that school would no longer welcome two year olds
by decreeing that grants would henceforth be made only for pupils three
years of age or older.

olds on a grand scale, American educators are advocating an even earlier start for reading than age three. Dr. Omar K. Moore at the Responsive Environments Foundation in Hamden, Connecticut, contends that children of two and three are better suited to begin reading than older children because learning is fun for infants and they are less upset by failure. Dr. Moore's recommendation arises from his successful instruction of two and three year olds using a "talking typewriter."

But the most sensational suggestions for early reading come from Glenn Doman, the director of the Institutes for the Achievement of Human Potential at Philadelphia in his book *How to Teach Your Baby to Read* (New York, 1963). The author claims that reading can be taught to one-year-old infants and, with a little extra effort, even to ten-month-old babies. The event that started Glenn Doman on his study of early reading is no less startling than his recommendations. Here is the story briefly.

Children with severe brain damage are apt to become human vegetables. One child, brain-damaged at birth, was admitted for neurosurgical examination at a New Jersey hospital. The chief neurosurgeon told the parents their little boy would never walk or talk, and the child would, therefore, be better off in an institution. The parents refused this advice and began searching for a source of hope.

Eventually, they were referred to the Institutes for the Achievement of Human Potential. Their son, by now aged three, was unable to move or talk. Following an evaluation of the child's brain injury, a treatment was prescribed and his parents were shown how to carry it out at home. They were told that if they adhered to the treatment, their son's condition might improve; and if his condition *did* improve, the therapy program would be revised accordingly.

The parents pursued their home program with almost religious zeal and their son's development proceeded in the following way: at the end of four months, the boy could crawl, and two months later he could say "Mummy" and "Daddy." Though the boy still couldn't walk at age five his speech and physical movements had advanced greatly. In fact, at this point, the puzzled specialists discovered that the parents had grossly overstepped the limits of the prescribed program. The parents had actually attempted to teach the child to read! And, as if this wasn't preposterous enough, they had succeeded! In fact, they had succeeded so well, the boy was reading better than normal children twice his age!

SURGICAL SURPRISES

Some of the procedures employed at the Institutes for the Achievement of Human Potential are drastic; for example, hemispherectomy, the surgical removal of an entire right or left half of a brain. The purpose of this operation is to prevent the diseased half from interfering with the proper functioning of the healthy half.

Following hemispherectomies, children receive special treatment to help them function in a more normal manner. However, the puzzling result of such brain removal was that the children treated were not only able to cope with life in an average manner, but were sometimes able to do so in an *above*-average manner; and at least one child with half his brain in a specimen jar was tabulated in the area of genius!

Then the specialists at the Institutes discovered they could sometimes normalize children without resorting to surgery, in fact, by employing physical therapy alone; and they eventually developed such an effective program of exercises that observers couldn't distinguish between a "half-brain" child, another who had been normalized solely by physical therapy, and a third, entirely normal child.

From this, the team of specialists concluded that neurological growth, though stopped by brain damage, could be regenerated by a program of mental and physical instruction. And they discovered that learning to read was a particularly powerful force in this regeneration. But imagine their surprise when, by this treatment, their child-patients occasionally developed greater mental ability than normal children! The team quite naturally wondered what was wrong with normal children.

One can almost hear the voice of William James echoing

his sage contention from the grave: "Compared with what we ought to be, we are only half awake. We are making use of only a small part of our physical and mental resources. Stating the thing broadly, the human individual thus lives far within his limits. He possesses powers of various sorts which he habitually fails to use."

Is there any valid reason, or necessity, for delaying a skill as simple as reading until a child reaches the grand age of six and a half? No one would suggest postponing—even if it were possible—a child's understanding of *spoken* English until the same age; yet the task of decoding *sounded* speech is similar to decoding *printed* speech. Printed speech is, after all, merely sound in a visible form, represented by commonly understood sound symbols. A child ultimately learns to interpret this code without help from his ears.

Whether a child *hears* speech or *sees* sound symbols representing that speech, he must still grasp meaning from whatever signal system is used. There is no evidence to show that the speech a child *hears* is initially and essentially easier for him to interpret than the speech he *sees*. Yet, by tradition, we encourage a child to begin decoding *spoken* words at age one, and *printed* words at age six and a half!

But perhaps learning to read at age one would impose too great a demand on a baby's vision. Not according to Dr. Burton White of Harvard. After experimenting with babies for several years and measuring their eye movements on TV monitor cameras, Dr. White and his associates concluded that by the time babies are four months old, they have developed visual-accommodation skills comparable to those of normal adults. Children are then able to focus near and far and track the path of moving objects.

Theoretically, therefore, Glenn Doman's suggested commencement of reading instruction at age ten months could be advanced six months. Whether or not we want so early a start to reading is another matter. But can children even *comprehend* speech at four months of age? Yes, according to Aaron Stern. In his book *The Making of a Genius* (Miami, 1971) the author discloses how, by an unusual program of instruction, he was able to teach his daughter to distinguish between the sound of four hundred words at five months of age. The baby, we are told, indicated recognition of the words by gesture.

A MOST UNUSUAL ADDRESS

Glenn Doman's book on brain-damaged children was published in 1963. Did its appearance trigger any revolution in educational methods? Not a bit. Witness a newspaper clipping dated February 28, 1973, reporting an address by a professor at the University of California's Berkeley campus and resident psychologist at the Institute for Human Learning. In this address, made at the annual meeting of the American Educationl Research Association, the speaker reported that a "massive number of children leaving the sixth grade have not learned to read and compute adequately." As a solution to the problem the professor urged that reading and mathematical instruction be delayed until grade 7—that is, ages twelve and thirteen! This wasn't a wild idea tossed around with giggles and rib poking in the teachers' room. This was a straight-faced proposal presented at a sedate gathering of people who influence American educational procedure.

Suppose, for a moment, this suggested delay were to be introduced (and crazier things have already happened in American education). We might expect a child to master "Run, Spot, run, as fast as you can," at about the time he reached dropout age.

The members of the American Educational Research Association are to be forgiven if they did not rise as a body and thump the table in frenzied agreement with the professor's proposal. My guess is they all felt too sick to move, because the amount of time and effort that has been spent on reading research over the years is staggering. More than *one thousand* reading-research studies are carried out *every year!* It is estimated that for every research study in mathematics *three* are done in reading.

RESEARCHING THE RESEARCHERS

What has this vast amount of reading research accomplished for North American children? Not much. Most of the findings have been ignored or distorted. The almost incredible story of oversight, inattention, illogic, and obstinacy in reading research is disclosed in Dr. Jean Chall's book, *Learning to Read—The Great Debate* (New York, 1967). This book, a detailed analysis of reading problems in the United States today, is a volume in the prestigious Carnegie Series in American Education. The work presents conclusions reached by Dr. Chall after visiting more than three hundred schools in the United States, England, and Scotland, monitoring classes from kindergarten to grade 3, and talking to teachers, school supervisors, and principals. In addition, Dr. Chall interviewed the authors of three widely used reading programs and one editor, and analyzed a total of twenty-two programs now in use. This project, from inception to published report, covered five years.

What does Dr. Chall have to say about present-day reading research techniques? She describes the research as "shockingly inconclusive"; it "says nothing consistently," and is "inadequate in both depth and scope." And the people who then interpreted this misinformation, we are told, "tended to over-generalize findings, especially those that fitted into prevailing educational views. They have paid only slight attention to studies that did not support these views. And they have tended to find all kinds of justification for their stands, even when faced with contradictory evidence." The crowning oversight, the author discloses, is that no one has troubled to correlate the many studies to learn what changes in reading instruction might seem prudent.

ACTION VERSUS INACTION

With confusion running wild for want of the ability to communicate, for want of scientific insight and the ability to form logical conclusions—indeed, for want of elemental professional honesty—it isn't surprising to hear a California professor suggest that reading instruction be checked until kids reach twelve and thirteen. But note: this is not an irresponsible plea. On the contrary—it is an honest, if unimaginative, attempt to cure an educational malignancy that vitiates North American schools. "It is staggering to believe," the professor sums up, "that they have learned virtually nothing of what was intended for them after the magnitude of their investment, and ours." This man is simply calling on his colleagues to admit they can't teach children to read and calculate before the ages of twelve and thirteen.

You may wonder, as I did, how children could possibly *enter* grade 6 if they couldn't read. How could children be promoted through five grades *without* the ability to read? Well, educational philosophy has changed a great deal in the last three decades; the importance of reading is now de-emphasized. In fact, the whole academic part of the curriculum in many states has been de-emphasized almost out of existence. Children learn to brush their teeth, to eat properly, to cook and sew, and in high school they now learn to type, to drive a car, how to behave on a date, how to select TV programs; they learn basket weaving, fly casting, hair grooming, and the philosophy of camping. In the 1973–74 term, two Kansas City (Kansas) high schools and a junior high school featured new facilities for teaching eighty courses, among them "Love and Loneliness" and "Bachelor Living" (the latter teaches boys how to stay well groomed and how to use a sewing machine). But, hold everything—New York University is now offering courses in "Bicycle Repair," "Folk-rock Guitar," and "Thoroughbred Thought" (which studies the fixing of odds in horse racing and how best to capitalize on them). Elsewhere we hear of children gaining an academic credit in a home-economics course by working part time in a supermarket!

In an educational climate of this sort, depreciating as it does the role of academic learning, there is far less reason for failing a child who can't read. Another factor that favors automatic promotion despite a child's poor reading ability (euphemistically termed "continuous progress") is the belief that his social development and sense of security might be upset if he were to drop a year behind his friends. So, rather than upset the child's emotional stability, he is advanced a grade where, everyone hopes, he will show greater interest and skill in reading.

These factors, then, are supposed to make delayed reading

both rational and socially acceptable. Indeed, with the elders
of the educational community nodding their heads in sage
approval and pointing out that older children learn more easily than younger children, the prescribed delay actually
seems to make sense.

By a distortion of logic, an even later delay than twelve and
thirteen years of age might seem advisable. During World
War II, the army's Special Training Units taught 85 per cent
of the illiterate trainees to read third-grade material in *eight
weeks*. To some, the army's commendable teaching success
might present a valid argument for delaying *everyone's* reading instruction until the age of eighteen.

The philosophy of delay in reading is indefensible. Delay,
offered as a solution to reading failure, is a sort of honorable
nondefeat achieved by strategic nonattempt—in short,
triumph by retreat. I believe that the only responsible action
to take with an ineffectual reading program is not to delay it,
but to *improve* it; and if you can't improve the program, then
for heaven's sake *replace* it.

Material has not the ability to make itself more or less difficult to learn. Educators alone control that, and they simplify
or complicate the material in the way they present it. *Manner*
of presentation, the key to easy learning, is the subject of the
next chapter.

CHAPTER 3

Colonel Sanders to the
Front of the Class, Please

When someone claims something can't be done, always ask: By what method?

To hear that a man fell 10,000 feet to earth from an airplane and was then able to pick himself up and walk away would be startling news only until you learned he had used a parachute. The method employed for any feat can make all the difference in the world—in this case, almost certainly the difference between life and death. To hear that two infants had learned to read in sixty days will probably seem startling, perhaps incredible, until the method used to teach them is fully understood.

THE STRANGE WORLD OF DENIS STOTT

The speed and ease with which a child learns to read is less a measure of the child than it is of the method used to teach him. If a reading expert tells you your child must be six and a half to begin reading, his estimate tells you more about his method than it tells you about your child.

In his book, *The Parent as Teacher* (Toronto, 1972), Dr. Denis H. Stott says, "Dogmas to the effect that a child cannot master the phonic [1] basis of reading until he reaches a mental age of six years are valid only so long as an unrealistic method of teaching phonics is used" (page 107). Dr. Stott, who teaches mentally retarded youngsters to read at the Centre for Education Disabilities, University of Guelph, Ontario, considers the term "mentally retarded" as meaningless. A child so described, he maintains, is really "learning-disabled." A learning-disabled child usually appears stupid in comparison with other children despite the great potential of his brain because of a quirk that isn't fully understood. A learning-disabled child requires more imaginative methods of instruction in order to unlock his potential.

When a learning-disabled child scores low on an IQ test, he is merely telling us how little he has managed to discover, by the usual methods, about the art of learning. The IQ does not tell us what he might accomplish if better methods— *unusual* methods—were used to teach him. In Dr. Stott's own words, "Until a child is using his mind, and using it aright, no one on earth can discover how much ability he has" (pages 4–5).

This holds for a normal child too; the method employed will determine how quickly and how well a child learns. With suitable instruction, a child's age, even his apparent low mentality, need not prohibit success. Elsewhere in his book, Dr. Stott reports the case of a Mongoloid boy, who by unique tuition, was able to read at the level of an average eight year old although the Mongoloid himself was only seven.[2]

When the teaching task is extremely difficult—as it is with "retarded" children—the importance of the teaching plan becomes immediately obvious. When teaching normal children, however, we commonly assume that teachers, by virtue of their special training, should teach easily and effectively. Teachers, on the other hand, more often regard those among

1. The interpretation of written English as sound.
2. A successful reading program for Mongoloids and other low-IQ children is described in "Severely Retarded People Can Learn to Read," by Renée Fuller in *Psychology Today* (October, 1974), 96–102.

them who teach effectively to be not teachers, but wizards; and the wizards—having a natural skill with learning strategies—teach well no matter what systems or materials are supplied them because they usually improve or replace the faulty elements in any program.

Unfortunately, creativity and imagination are no more common among teachers than among any other group of people, so the majority of teachers are not able to improve or replace ineffective reading programs—even if they were able to recognize one. Small wonder reading continues to be the number-one teaching headache when unsuspecting teachers are given packaged reading programs containing built-in problems rather than built-in solutions. Can guaranteed success be built into a program? Dr. Maria Montessori provided such a model.

THE FIRST LADY OF EDUCATION

When Dr. Montessori was appointed director of the State Orthophrenic School for mentally defective children in Rome, 1899, she invented a program of instruction and a variety of teaching aids that permitted defective children to achieve the same level of academic skill as normal healthy children. This startling success led Dr. Montessori to wonder why normal children performed no better than they did, so she set herself the goal of improving education, and opened, in 1906, her own school for infants: the first link in an educational chain that now circles the globe.

The Montessori books and equipment, all tested and proved, permit almost anyone to teach groups of young children, and teach them well. The Montessori fail-proof, teacher-proof method of instruction exemplifies the sort of program teachers need if learning is to improve.

Until educationalists provide tested and proved programs of instruction, schools are likely to continue producing great numbers of dropouts and an even greater number of uneducated stay-ins. A lengthy newspaper report, dated February 5, 1973, reads: "U.S. is facing a reading crisis." The report begins by declaring that five million job hunters can't even read the help-wanted ads. This provocative statement isn't the creation of an enterprising reporter but the sober assertion of the National Reading Center; its next glum revelation: "In junior colleges, 30–50 per cent of entering students need reading help." *This is at age seventeen and eighteen!*

But wait. If you think *that* news is bad, it's because you haven't heard the proposed solution. The National Reading Center, in collaboration with the Safeway food chain, the National Dairy Council, and the Milk Industry Foundation, hopes to popularize reading by imprinting milk cartons with messages such as, "Milk, your child's key to nutrition; books, your child's key to learning," accompanied by a cartoon showing a mother and child entering a library. A spokesman for the National Reading Center said, "Now we're trying to interest cereal manufacturers in carrying a comparable message."

Should we really expect messages on food containers to improve faulty teaching methods? If this is the highest degree of problem-solving skill educationalists can demonstrate, then learning to read may soon become a night-school course for working adults.

Am I kidding? It's already a fact! In *Tomorrow's Illiterates,* (ed., Charles C. Walcutt [Boston, 1961]), Helen R. Lowe reports the case of Arthur Young, a painter and carpenter who, after four years of high school, received a diploma maintaining he had "satisfactorily completed the curriculum requirements prescribed by the Board of Education for the High School and is entitled to this Diploma." His final report card gave him the top marks, H for Honor, in English throughout his senior year.

Just one small detail marred Arthur's record of academic excellence. He couldn't read. Shakespeare? Hell, no! He couldn't read street signs, traffic directions, menus, or letters from his family (which he couldn't answer anyway). And in his own trades as painter and carpenter, "he could not read the mixing directions on a can of paint or the label on a shipment of sheet rock. He had been cheated and swindled in various ways as a consequence of his inability to read."

You don't believe it? Neither did every publisher's reader

who checked the manuscript for that chapter of *Tomorrow's Illiterates,* so the editor felt obliged to add a footnote stating that he had personally examined a copy of the report card.

Elsewhere we learn of a college admissions officer who was obliged to assign a clerk to help high-school graduates fill in their admission forms because many applicants couldn't read or write.[3]

Schools are becoming more like young people's clubs where credits are given for subjects such as arts, crafts, music, dance, gymnastics, swimming, deportment, social awareness, etiquette, personality, and leadership. Granted, the arts, the social graces, and sports are important, but if children don't learn to read, to write, and to compute quickly and accurately, then schools are merely producing pleasant, personable ignoramuses.

Everyone passes; no one fails; everyone gets a diploma; scholastic dreams come true. But the honorary graduation of uneducated children can never be anything more than a shameful hoax on pupils and parents alike. What is the position of school children who cannot read and write effectively? Arther S. Trace, Jr.[4] writes of them, "They may be budding young unemployables, and may well be on the way to forming their own little pockets of poverty."

A UNESCO-sponsored survey by the International Association for the Evaluation of Educational Achievement discovered in 1973 that ten-year-old American children can't read as well as ten year olds in nine other countries. And Louis Harris estimates from his polls that nineteen million American adults are illiterate, and another seven million children under the age of sixteen are doomed to a life of illiteracy.

Teachers have unions to protect their interests; why shouldn't parents? Parents finance schools through their taxes; they have a right to expect good service for their money. One effective way of inspiring schools to better performance was introduced by the Revised Code of the Committee of Council on Education of 1862. London schools of that day received grants based solely on what their pupils

3. Aaron Stern, *The Making of a Genius* (Miami, 1971), p. 164.
4. Arther S. Trace, Jr., *Reading without Dick and Jane* (Chicago, 1965).

learned. Money was granted only for those children who could pass the examinations set by the council.[5]

PARENTS FIGHT BACK

Children today are just as clever as children were in the past, but they are less ambitious. Thanks to the advent of television, our life style has become more passive, more sedentary. We have developed powerful sitting muscles. The cop-out, dropout philosophy virtually applauds indolence. "Doin' your thing" all too often means doing little or nothing, so when low motivation outside of school is matched by low motivation inside school, the stage is set for a horrendous drop in academic standards—exactly what we have.

Two innovators, Steven Daniels [6] and Allan Harrison,[7] have shown how learning can be accelerated when pupils are properly motivated. In fact, children were so fascinated by Allan Harrison's method, they sometimes fretted when holidays kept them out of school, wanted to attend school even when ill, and preferred doing homework to playing with friends. Can we wonder that his pupils learned twice as much as other children?

Elsewhere, children sometimes learn so little that parents band together in protest. One group, the Parent Action League, has challenged the methods used in Toronto schools, and is militantly campaigning for a change in teaching techniques because their children can't read and write.

When a member of the league tested children from grades 7, 8, and 9 (aged thirteen to sixteen) on the spelling of forty-one common one- or two-syllable words, she discovered an appalling level of incompetance. Of the 469 students tested, here are the number who were *not* able to spell this sampling of words: *Bob*—31, *stork*—60, *quilt*—116, *scuffle*—244, *whiff*—405.

5. Tessa Blackstone, *A Fair Start: The Provision of Pre-School Education* (London, 1971), p. 23.

6. Steven Daniels, *How 2 Gerbils 20 Goldfish 200 Games 2,000 Books and I Taught Them How to Read* (Philadelphia, 1971).

7. Allan Harrison, *How to Teach Children Twice as Much* (New York, 1973).

Another group in Wichita, Kansas, became so disgusted with the poor quality of education their children were receiving that they finally threw up their hands and founded their own school—Wichita Collegiate. Graduates of that school average ninety points higher than the national average (485) on college entrance exams.[8]

Whether a child learns, *how much* he learns, *with what ease* he learns, and *how long* he remembers the material taught him provide far greater comment on the worth of a teaching program than they do on a child's capacity for learning. Teaching a group of forty children need be no more difficult than teaching a group of ten provided the program is *designed* for forty children. One hundred seventy-five years ago in London, England, a solitary teacher, Joseph Lancaster (1778–1838), routinely taught one thousand children to read and write in about two months, and even one child in just three weeks.[9]

When a suitable teaching program is invented—and I'm convinced it will be—children in small or large groups will learn to read in sixty days, and will, during the same period, learn elementary mathematics and some geography; their interest will be roused in several other subjects, and they will have a whale of a time throughout the procedure. And anyone who says "Can't be done" would have said the same of teaching a two year old to read in sixty days.

For the small amount of learning that currently takes place in schools each day, they might better be thought of as child-care centers with an educational atmosphere. The total amount of knowledge children now acquire during a day should, rightfully, be learned in less than two hours. Children could then be permitted to spend the rest of their day out of school pursuing their own interests. And, with stimulating methods of instruction, we shouldn't be surprised if children voluntarily spent some of their free time tracking down answers to questions raised in class.

Methods of teaching that ignore childish fascinations and

8. Robert Love, *How to Start Your Own School* (New York, 1973).
9. *The Life and Writings of DeWitt Clinton* (Baker & Scribner, 1849), p. 318.

cravings are doomed to failure or, at best, to only partial success. If Dr. Stott had ignored the special needs of his learning-disabled children and had attempted to teach them by the usual methods, he would, of course, have met with the usual failure. However, Dr. Stott was more resourceful than that. He contrived an *unusual* program of reading instruction, one so simple, interesting, and enjoyable that it didn't *permit* learning-disabled children to fail.

When imaginative teaching methods are employed, the boundaries of learning can be stretched to a remarkable extent. In a converse manner, unimaginative methods restrict learning. The Morphett and Washburne report, published in 1931, fixed reading commencement at age six and a half. The report was, however, merely the sour custard atop a pudding of general educational stupidity.

GAMES RESEARCHERS PLAY

In the 1920s, many psychologists believed that children were unable to read before they were six and a half because the various systems of their bodies—muscular, circulatory, and nervous—were not sufficiently developed to meet the demands of reading.

Most babies demonstrate specific skills at specific ages. For example, a normal child begins to crawl at five or six months of age, sits unaided at around ten months, and walks at fifteen months. These ages and achievements hold true for the majority of children.

Though these earliest physical skills can be delayed in various ways, they cannot be hastened very much. For a child to crawl, his muscles and nervous system must reach a certain point of development. Similarly, sitting unaided and walking require further muscular development or readiness. No matter how much a child is urged or otherwise motivated, he won't be able to master these skills until his body reaches the stage of maturation necessary for that particular skill. *Maturation* simply means the coming to ripeness or maturing of a body system.

When educators noticed that some children had difficulty

learning to read at the beginning of grade 1, they began looking around for the reason. It didn't occur to them that the
method of teaching was at fault. Instead, they adapted the
maturation theory to reading.

The marriage of education to physiology wasn't a hasty
one. The courtship began at the turn of the century, with
John Dewey as one of the principal matchmakers. Dewey,
you will recall, believed that the human body was not equal
to the task of reading and writing before the age of eight. The
link between physiology and learning was strengthened by
another prominent educational psychologist of the period,
G. Stanley Hall, who promoted the doctrine of recapitulation.
According to this law, the individual in his development
passes through stages similar to those the whole race has
passed, and in the same order.

Biologically, this makes sense, because every human possesses the gills of fish at one point in his embryonic development, and each of us carries around the remnant of a tail
represented by the coccyx. Hall's theory profoundly affected
the thinking of his students, some of whom ultimately became prominent themselves in education: Frederick Kuhl-
mann, Lewis Terman, and Arnold Gesell.

Of the three, Gesell, a physician, became the most influen-
tial, both through his own prodigious work and writing and
through that of his students at the Gesell Institute.

GESELL'S READING LEGACY

Arnold Gesell put forward the idea of "neural ripening"
and "intrinsic growth" as an explanation of, and a guide to,
children's learning patterns. When children experienced difficulty reading at age six, Gesell reasoned, it was because
"reading maturation" didn't occur until age six and a half.

No one, including Gesell, seems to have considered that
reading maturation was a quality to *develop* in a child rather
than to wait for, and so the unproductive habit of waiting
became common practice. The Morphett-Washburne study of
Winnetka school children in 1931 championed procrasti-
nation and drew attention to the bonuses of waiting. "It

seems safe to state," the authors declared, "that by postponing the teaching of reading until children reach a mental age level of six and a half years, teachers can greatly decrease the chances of failure and discouragement and can correspondingly increase their efficiency." [10]

In addition to being superintendant of the Winnetka school system, Carleton Washburne was also a leader of the Progressive Education Movement; and when Washburne spoke, the educational community paid attention. As if any further support was needed for the Morphett-Washburne proposals, their recommendations were also in locked step with the published belief of the National Society for the Study of Education—namely, that the first half of grade 1 should be spent preparing children for reading.

Not surprisingly, therefore, Morphett and Washburne's conclusions based on a "scientific" study, drew an eager band of educators and psychologists to their ranks. But Morphett and Washburne's personal triumph was the nation's loss, and for the next forty years their report addled the thinking of many educators, arrested their imagination, and discouraged experimentation in reading.

SYSTEMS KNIT WITH WOOLLY THOUGHT

According to Morphett and Washburne, mental age played a much greater role in determining the correct age for beginning reading than did IQ.[11] In other words, an extremely bright three year old having a mental age of four (IQ 133) would not be able to read for another two years or so. This reliance on mental age rather than chronological age opened still another drawer in the chest of reading pseudo science. By 1936, every first-grade teacher in Winnetka had a chart to help her eliminate guesswork in assessing a child's mental age. The content of the charts lengthened each year

10. M. V. Morphett and C. Washburne, "When Should Children Begin to Read?," *Elementary School Journal*, XXXI (March, 1931), 496–503.

11. IQ rating is determined by the formula: mental age × 100 divided by chronological or actual age. Therefore a child aged five with the mental age of a ten year old would have an IQ of 200, whereas a ten year old with a mental age of five would have an IQ of 50.

as educators sought to pinpoint the week—who knows, perhaps the very day—a child was ready for reading. Some of the signs to watch for were listed in the *Thirty-eighth Yearbook of the National Society for the Study of Education* (Bloomington, Ill., 1939). According to the list, a child who had reached the mental age of six and a half would display a keen interest in reading, would have reasonably wide experience, facility in the use of ideas, ability to solve abstract problems, a reasonable range of vocabulary, emotional stability, good health, vision, hearing, and normal speech organs.

Frankly, many *adults* I meet can't fill these requirements except for having normal speech organs. We could hardly blame the teachers if, after consulting their charts, they sought further guidance from an Ouija board.

KEEPERS OF THE MYTH

Incredible though it seems, some books in the 1960s were still taking the mental-age doctrine seriously, thanks mainly to psychologists of the forties and fifties who continued to endorse the maturation concept of the twenties but in an updated jargon, "organismic moment" and "teachable moment." These almost poetic expressions lent considerable grandeur to a feather-brained idea. The term in use today is *reading readiness.*

Perhaps the seventies will see a final abandonment of the "readiness" myth. But if so, it will have to be later in the seventies, because Robert E. Silverman's textbook, *Psychology* published in 1972 (New York), tells university students that "psychologists are now able to specify the average age of readiness for the learning of various tasks. For example, reading readiness usually occurs at the age of six."

A complete branch of psychology is devoted to the study of learning and the influences that favor or thwart it. Thousands of experiments have been performed with various animals to discover some of the secrets of the learning process. Most, if not all, of the findings shed some light on the way humans learn.

In writing *Psychology,* Dr. Silverman drew on the content

of 1,200 books, articles, and monographs. If, after studying this astonishing collection of literature on a subject in which human learning plays a major role, Dr. Silverman *still* thinks reading readiness occurs at age six, we should hardly be surprised if misinformed teachers believe it too.

Perpetuation of the "readiness" myth has no parallel in the world of science since the Flat Earth Society disbanded. One curious research report concluded that reading readiness occurred when a child was 47 inches tall, weighed 47 pounds, had a mental age of six and a half, had seven little bones in his wrist, and a 26-pound grip! [12]

And so, parents—misguided by teachers, in turn misguided by educators and psychologists—who in every respect provide the best for their children, restrict their children's early education and entertainment to the cultural limits of TV, and leave reading instruction to the last moment permitted by law. (No law forbids a child's education *before* age six, though a law prevents its delay later than six—and five in England.)

The compulsory schooling law, enacted to guarantee a basic education for every child, was, unfortunately, another factor that discouraged imaginative teaching. When children were obliged by law to appear in school every day, what need was there to capture their interest? As a consequence, teaching took on the manner of pouring information into children as if they were empty bottles, testing to see if there was enough "inside," and if there was, moving the bottles along the conveyor to higher grades for further increments.

The attitude that prompted and supported this kind of teaching was not the sort requiring imagination. Not surprisingly, the "doctrine of postponement" as it was known, became widely accepted in the 1920s. Teachers were advised to wait until the pupils ripened, at which time, teachers were assured, reading would become effortless. Incredibly enough, this naïve idea continues to dominate modern curriculums.

12. Reported by Sybil Terman and Charles C. Walcutt, *Reading: Chaos and Cure* (New York, 1958), p. 120.

If the effectiveness of teaching methods has *not* improved during the last fifty years (and this seems to be the case), what have educationalists been getting paid for during this period? Must it be left to amateurs to solve educational problems? The more I learn of educational malpractice and the more I see of the vast amount of work to be done, the more I begin to feel like the new immigrant to America who wrote home glumly reporting that the streets were *not* paved with gold, that some streets weren't even paved, and, what's more, it was *his* job to pave them!

READING READINESS

The philosophy of "reading readiness" is merely a convenient excuse to exonerate poor teaching programs. Though I question the value of teaching a child to read earlier than age two, there can no longer be any doubt that it is possible. You will probably find that whenever you are ready to teach your own child to read, he'll be ready too.

When educators begin putting together some imaginative reading programs, they too will discover that children are more than ready to read in kindergartens and nursery schools, and that they will do so with speed and accuracy.

Dr. Glenn McCracken describes some of the farcical methods used to assess readiness for reading and their ruinous long-term effect on children's academic careers.[13] Children are given picture books and crayons and asked to mark their illustrations appropriately. For example, they are asked to underline the smallest squirrel in a group of four and, in another test, to draw a line from a little boy to a house and to put a mark on a donkey that looks angry! Because it occurred to me that Dr. McCracken might be ridiculing only the more obscure tests still in use, I contacted the Education Clinic at the Ottawa Board of Education and spoke to the head of that department, Margaret Hill. "Dr. McCracken's example of test projects," she assured me, "are, unfortunately consistent with those commonly used." As it is Mrs. Hill's job to try to repair

13. Glenn McCracken, "Reading Readiness in Theory and Practice," in *Tomorrow's Illiterates*, ed. Charles C. Walcutt (Boston, 1961), pp. 71–84.

the damage done by poor reading instruction, this teacher has little time for nonsense techniques. She then described other widely used tests in which a child's readiness for reading is judged by his ability to discriminate between like and unlike pictures and on his ability to manipulate a pencil!

What on earth has manipulating a pencil to do with reading? For want of such ability, an armless child would have to be considered incurably illiterate. Eve and Jean, neither of whom could manipulate a pencil prior to reading, would have failed the manipulation test. Had I been guided by a belief in such tests, this book would not have been written.

Elsewhere, we hear of a teacher who tested reading readiness by striking various notes on the piano and asking pupils whether the notes were similar or different. This test would assign less reading aptitude to a brilliant, though tone-deaf, child than it would to a blind child with a discriminating ear.

These curious tests would be comical but for the hundreds of thousands of youngsters whose education is hampered each year because of absurd predictions based on their use. But even the widely used American School Reading Readiness Test, though proposing less bizarre exercises, furnishes an equally unreliable assessment of children's reading potential—proved by the performance of pupils in New Castle, Pennsylvania. Predictions based on the test bore little relationship to children's actual reading accomplishments at the end of grade 1.[14]

READY WHEN YOU ARE, COLONEL

If anyone had contended ten years ago that Mr. and Mrs. Average American could be induced to hop in the car and drive to a neighborhood kitchen for fried chicken (and by the bucketful at that!), he would have been thought mad. Housewives and chefs have been cooking fried chicken for a long time. Some of them may have prepared their chicken even better than Colonel Sanders does; but much more than a tasty recipe is needed to make multitudes venture forth at all

14. Glenn McCracken, *The Right to Learn* (Chicago, 1974).

hours in quest of finger-lickin' delights. The magic ingre-
dients in the Colonel's success aren't in his chicken recipe at
all; they're in his knowledge of showmanship, salesmanship,
and systemization for maximum transfer value. When you
order Kentucky Fried Chicken from a franchised dealer, you
expect the same quality of food whether you order it in
Alaska or Florida, and thanks to Colonel Sanders, you *get* it.
Here's how it's done.

Let's suppose you wanted to open a franchised chicken
store in your town or city. After the paperwork had been
taken care of, you would be told a proved way to select a
good location for your store. You would be given proved
plans for a store layout, ones guaranteeing efficient production and serving. You would be shown a proved method for
hiring the right sort of staff. You would be instructed in
proved methods of cooking and seasoning the chickens, and
in proved management techniques. Finally, you would be
supplied with low-cost chickens. National advertising, han-
dled by the parent company, would then attract customers to
your store.

Nothing is left to chance. Every detail in a franchised program is puzzled out and solved for you. This is the promised,
proved, predictable success that comes with franchised deal-
ership. With plenty of effort (the only other requirement besides investment capital), you could then watch the profits
mount in a promised, proved, and predictable way.

What a contrast to the uncertain, unproved, unpredictable
reading programs teachers must use! In my opinion, any
method of school instruction less artful than that which guar-
antees the triumphant and profitable presentation of chicken
carcasses is unacceptable when teaching one of the most important skills children will ever need.

Colonel Sanders and Maria Montessori seem an incongru-
ous match; one solved a complex marketing problem, the
other a complex educational problem. But both solved their
problems in a manner others could easily employ; their solutions could be transferred to other people in other places.
Each said, in effect, "Take these materials, follow these in-

structions I have carefully worked out, and you will achieve these stated results."

We need child-tested, child-approved, packaged educational programs featuring quick, easy learning with success *guaranteed*—guaranteed, that is, whether children are taught by a gifted and experienced teacher or by an inexperienced or untalented one.

I may be accused of wanting to see children educationally processed with the sameness that characterized Colonel Sanders's chickens, but this would only be to confuse *method*, which is concerned with quick, effortless learning, and *content*, concerned with the material to be learned. Conformity of belief is not the goal, but rather consistency of teaching excellence.

CHAPTER 4

Ordeal by Classroom

OUR WARRING NEIGHBORS

At the time of our reading program, I was frequently awakened in the morning by the sound of gunfire. Gang warfare in Ottawa, the small, quiet seat of Canadian government? No, just a small, bloodless war waged by a lone gunman driving slowly around in a half-ton pickup truck, firing blank cartridges to frighten away flocks of blackbirds, pigeons, and starlings. The area under contest by bird and man was a 12-acre experimental crop of corn on a 1,200-acre farm lying wholly within the city limits. This land, the government's Central Experimental Farm, adjoins three sides of the lot on which our apartment building stands.

The children's nursery lies a mile away near another corner of the farm. Rather than shuttle to and from the nursery on city streets, I drive through the farm's pleasant shaded laneways—Ash Lane (lined with ash trees), to Cow Lane, then to Morningside Lane. Not surprisingly, the girls' vocabulary has become a mixture of rural and urban words. *Barn* is as common to them as *apartment*. Cows, pigs, sheep, and bulls are not mere illustrations in books, but real animals to watch—and sometimes to touch—no less real than the police cars, ambulances, and fire engines that frequently speed along the main arterial route beneath our window.

THE FALSE START

Our reading program had a false start. I had tried to teach the children reading five months earlier, but stopped when the weakness of my method became apparent. The technique had been described in a British newspaper in 1964—children could be taught to read by periodically displaying or "flashing" cards with words printed in large letters. In this way, children learned to recognize whole words. Reading was as simple as that!

Well, I knew nothing about reading instruction. If this was the way to go about it, then fine. I printed the girls' names on cards 5½ inches by 8 inches, and sure enough, after the cards had been flashed a few times, the children had been able to recognize their names. Learning by this method seemed an easy matter, so during the next few weeks cards with **Daddy, Elke, Jan, Thomas,** and **Catherine** were added. But now, with several words to choose from, the children had begun guessing. Reading, not guessing, was our goal, so I stopped the lessons.

At the time, I didn't know the method we used had a name. I learned later that it had several, among them "reading for meaning," "word," "word recognition," "whole word," "look-say," and even "natural." Five months later, when we began what was to be our successful program, I simply used the method by which I myself had been taught: one bearing the awesome title, 'systematic phonics with blending."

THE PHONIC METHOD

In the phonic method, the *sounds* of the letters rather than their names are learned. For example, instead of saying "ay," "bee," "see" (for *a, b, c*) a child is taught to say "ah," "buh," "kuh." [1] Having learned to sound these three letters, a child might then look at the word *cab,* and voice the three letters quickly enough to form a blended sound which his ears would catch and recognize as *cab.* (*Cab* was, in fact, one of the first words my children learned.)

Critics of the phonic method claim there are too many irregularities in English pronunciation to assign sounds to individual letters or groups of letters. The example most frequently given to support this view is the many sounds represented by the letters *-ough,* as seen in *cough, tough, bough, though.* Word puzzles such as *phtholognyrrh* seem to support the critics' claims. How would *you* pronounce the manufactured word *phtholognyrrh?* It's pronounced "turner"; the *phth-* (sounded as a *t*) has been taken from the word *phtisic;* the *-olo-* (sounded as *ur*) comes from "colonel"; the *-gn-* is from *gnat;* and the *-yrrh* from *myrrh.* And, wily George Bernard Shaw defied anyone to correctly pronounce his special combination of letters *ghoti.* They are sounded *fish* for, as Shaw disclosed, *gh-* is taken from *enough,* the *-o-* from *women,* and the *-ti* from *nation.*

These phonic high jinks push the apparent lawlessness of our language to its extreme but give no hint to the many simple phonic rules that make word deciphering easy and accurate.

Learning to read by the phonic method is slower at first than by the whole-word method because children are obliged to learn at least a few phonic rules before they can begin decoding words. Had I taught Eve and Jean by the

---

1. A detailed description of these sounds is given later.

whole-word method, they might have memorized two words a day right from the start, and perhaps fourteen words by the end of the first week; whereas in reality, using phonics, they were able to decode only five words at the end of seven days.

But when children have learned the sounds of the letters, this knowledge can be applied to *most* words, like a key. Knowing the letter sounds, therefore, has transfer value, and reading vocabularies grow quickly as a result of it. Consequently, Eve and Jean were able to read 186 words at the end of sixty days instead of the 120 they might possibly have read by proceeding at the steady rate of two whole words a day—completely ignoring the thousands of phonically regular words the children might have decoded had I troubled to present these words to them.

But, besides the *quantity* of words the girls could read, there is the important matter of reading *quality*. Eve and Jean could read every word singly or as part of a sentence, whereas children who learn to read whole words are often obliged to study the accompanying illustration for help in recognizing a word, or else try to find a clue in the words on each side of it.

NONSENSE READERS

After our false start with the name cards, I put reading instruction aside. However, my interest was instantly revived four months later on discovering the children, books open before them, pretending to read aloud from the printed page, when in fact they were merely inventing a story to fit the illustrations. That did it! The humor of their performance seemed only to heighten the unacceptability of it. I resolved to teach the girls to read soon. But how?

I didn't know there were twenty different ways to teach reading—among them: "systematic phonics," "integrated phonics," "phonically enriched basals," "reading experience programs," and such. Indeed, had I known of these complexities in advance, our program wouldn't have been attempted, and Eve and Jean would probably still be sitting on the floor today inventing stories to fit text they couldn't read.

Protected thus by ignorance, I began looking for a quick, easy method to teach reading. The method *had* to be quick for reasons mentioned earlier: my busy schedule and my limited patience with children. I had taught before, but only adults, and the subject wasn't academic, but art. However, as an education buff, I had already developed an unusual teaching system, the techniques of which seemed to offer a solution to our present reading problem.

UNILINGUAL TROOPS

From 1962 to 1969 I lived in Europe writing fiction that didn't sell and supported myself by drawing caricatures at U.S. and Canadian military bases in France and Germany.

I noted a peculiarity. Although troops lived abroad for as long as four years, few learned more than twenty words of the host country's language despite their purchase and study of language-learning materials. True, the North Americans' shopping, recreational, and social needs were filled chiefly by the military base, and the troops usually lived separately from the nationals; but insulated living really didn't justify such little language learning.

What was the barrier to learning? Boredom. Learning a foreign language from materials rather than by conversation is extremely boring despite the promises of quick, effortless progress made by manufacturers of language courses.

I wondered if there might be a way to make learning another language genuinely quick and easy. Repetition of study matter, the key to most learning, is also the key to boredom. Yet games thrive on repetition. For example, the game Monopoly is, basically, just a routine, repeated circuit of the playing board plus an entertaining involvement with money and real estate; and although learning the names of the "properties" is not a goal of the players, the streets are often so well memorized that players can recite them in correct sequence without looking at the board. If nonsense material could be easily learned by playing games, why couldn't "sense" or "useful" material?

I adapted a few French words to a simple table game and

invited friends to play it. They learned the words so quickly, I was prompted to begin devising a complete language course based on the use of games. The method, completed five years later, permits a beginner to gain easy use of basic French in just forty-four hours of involvement—half of which time is spent playing games.[2]

JOHN LOCKE'S LEGACY

I was surprised to learn later that John Locke, the English philosopher, had recommended a games approach to learning back in 1693. In *Some Thoughts Concerning Education,* Locke says: "I have always had a fancy that learning might be made a play and recreation to children; and that they might be brought to desire to be taught if it were proposed to them as a thing of honour, credit, delight, and recreation, or as a reward for doing something else. . . . There may be dice and playthings, with the letters on them to teach children the alphabet by playing; and twenty other ways may be found, suitable to their particular tempers, to make this kind of learning a sport to them. . . . I have therefore thought, that if playthings were fitted to this purpose, as they are usually [fitted] to none, contrivances might be made to teach children to read, whilst they thought they were only playing . . . cheat [them] into it if you can." Locke goes on to describe how vowels and consonants might be affixed to the faces of dice.

To date, only toy manufacturers have seen the merit of Locke's suggestion; so the most intriguing devices for learning are found not in schools, but in toy stores—and Locke's alphabetical dice, called *Spill and Spell,* are among them.

AND NOW, THE BOGEYMEN

No criticism is made of preschool reading instruction when it is given at a Montessori nursery. However, similar tuition given at home is often viewed with alarm. Parents are some-

2. S. Ledson, *The FUNdamental French Language Course* (Ottawa, 1971).

times made to feel that their unprofessional meddling with the child's delicate intellect is an act almost as reprehensible as performing a lobotomy on the kitchen table. Let's consider some frequently voiced fears.

"Some teachers tell you not to teach your child to read at home." Indeed, some teachers do, and teachers, like everyone else, are entitled to their opinion. But we must remember that though teachers have a great deal of firsthand experience in teaching reading, they are, in matters of theory, largely dependent on what authorities tell them. And, as the record shows, they have often been told nonsense.

"A child who can already read will be bored in school." There are many reasons why a child might be bored in school. It could be because of the teacher, the subject, the season, or something else. But the child most vulnerable to boredom is the one who has lost interest in schoolwork simply because he finds the work difficult and does it badly. If, because of his early reading ability, a child finds schoolwork unchallenging, he can be given an enriched curriculum or be advanced to the next grade. Any teacher worthy of the name should welcome an opportunity to take part in the progress of an exceptional child. And if a teacher is too lacking in spirit to rise to such a challenge, then it will probably be a tedious year for the whole class.

"A bright child will have difficulty adjusting throughout his entire schooling." Assuredly, a bright child will have need to adjust, though no one can predict how difficult the adjustment may be. Learning to adapt and adjust is an important part of growing up, and adapting, as with most things, improves with the doing. All children have problems, and, I suspect, if each of these problems were sorted out and assigned a value of distress based on the child's assessment of its importance, we might find all problems about equally distressing to their owners. Children consider themselves too fat, too thin, too tall, too short, having too large noses, unsightly freckles, acne, poor posture, too little strength, too few stylish clothes, large ears or feet, breasts the wrong size, and so on.

From my observation, children who excell in school without developing an inflated opinion of their own personal worth usually secure the respect and friendship of their classmates.

In his article "Education of the Exceptional," [3] Samuel Alexander Kirk, professor of Special Education, University of Arizona, Tucson, concludes: "Research on the personal adjustment of gifted and handicapped children (other than the socially or emotionally disturbed) has not shown the probability of maladjustment to be as great as 'common sense' would indicate. It was once assumed, for example, that a gifted child would show exceptional talent in some area but would be abnormal in social relations. This myth has long been discarded; studies over a period of years have shown that the extremely gifted (children with IQs of 140 and above) were better adjusted than the average, personally, and socially, in school and in later life."

There are so many excuses voiced for delaying children's reading that it is impossible to comment on them all. Some people claim it is more important to rouse children's natural curiosity, as if by learning to read, curiosity is somehow diminished or inhibited!

Early reading has also been said to rob a child of his childhood, ignoring the fact that a child who can read stories for himself is getting much more out of childhood than a child who is dependent for his stories on the presence and mood of an adult. Eight months after their reading lessons began, Eve and Jean read sixty-two books in a two-week period, fifty-six of which they had never seen before. How many parents could find the time to read a similar amount to their children and, incidentally, find the patience to read them *The Three Little Pigs* exuberantly for the tenth time?

Childhood is a time of wondrous discovery. Children yearn to participate in what they see going on around them and to know more about it. Being able to read helps them do so. By reading, children enjoy larger spheres of interest just as adult readers participate more fully in life than adult illiterates.

3. *Encyclopaedia Britannica*, 15th ed., *Macropaedia*, vol. 6, pp. 431–434.

THE BAD TRIP

A tightly scheduled educational program *can*, of course, rob a child of childhood, as it did for John Stuart Mill, who at four had Greek lessons during the day and arithmetic in the evening. Mill was rarely allowed books of interest to children (nor was he allowed toys!). The lad had *not* been taught to read for pleasure but rather for the acquisition of knowledge, and he was then goaded to learn at an astonishing rate.

Mill's learning experience is not likely to be emulated. Who would want it for their child? The acquisition of facts doesn't guarantee happiness or wisdom; nor, for that matter, does a child's speedy passage through school. If a child is promoted an extra grade as a result of early reading skill, fine; but *learning,* not promotion, is supposed to be the purpose of schooling, and an important part of that education involves getting along with others.

Some parents have paid dearly for the privilege of raising a brilliant child. Mill's father paid an exorbitant price, for though the son respected his father greatly, he was never able to feel any real affection for him. We should hardly be surprised that young Mill suffered a nervous breakdown at the age of twenty. The case of John Stuart Mill properly serves as a warning that moderation in all things also applies to early education. However, the delay of reading until age six is not moderation either, but rather, I submit, an insult to the human intellect.

Capable, knowledgeable children soon gain a level of self-confidence that permits them to tackle problems in a bouyant manner. They think "can" instead of "can't" and, consequently, often achieve goals unattainable by others. Such children have a long (a lifetime!) history of conquering problems. Past successes permit them to take occasional failure in their stride, and having survived past failures, they know they will survive future failures.

Possession of early reading skill is a giant step toward ultimate high academic performance. Indeed, a child's success at reading is his *first* academic success, so a precedent for later scholastic excellence is already established in the early years. But the most compelling reason for teaching a child to read before he begins school is that it provides the only known guarantee he will become a proficient, venturesome reader.

BAD NEWS

Despite its ruinous effect on national reading standards, the whole-word method continues to be used in four out of five schools. The origin of the whole-word method, how it gained popularity, and how it defies eviction from schools is a long story, one well told in Samuel L. Blumenfeld's *The New Illiterates*. Arther S. Trace, Jr., has coined the expression "programmed retardation" to describe the inhibiting influence of the whole-word method on literacy, and in his book *Reading without Dick and Jane* he reveals the greater financial rewards to be reaped by publishing reading programs that don't work too well.

There is small profit in easy literacy, big profit in illiteracy. Children who have been taught restricted reading vocabularies (common practice with whole-word programs) can't read ordinary books; they haven't memorized enough words to do so. Instead, they must rely on the obliging publisher to produce a wealth of books (including many children's classics) written in the restricted idiot-level vocabulary [4] his own reading program teaches.

Despite a host of small groups, and two international organizations (the Council for Basic Education, and the Reading Reform Foundation) [5] urging the expulsion of whole-word instruction from classrooms, the method maintains its position

4. Studies made in 1957 by Mildred C. Templin and in 1964 by Wilbur S. Ames indicate that an average grade-two pupil has a speech vocabulary of twenty thousand words; yet whole-word reading programs (commonly called basals) teach a child to read only about eight hundred words by the end of grade two. And four years later, on completion of grade six, an average child will still be reading only five thousand words. Any eleven year old whose reading is limited to one fourth the speech vocabulary of a seven year old might just as well be an idiot as far as the printed word is concerned.

5. Addresses on p. 207.

of supremacy (sometimes as if magically endowed). For example, though Mary Johnson wrote a complete book—citing names, dates, test results, and press comments—exposing the harmful effects of the whole-word method on reading skill in Winnipeg schools,[6] that method continues to dominate curriculums there!

The total devastating effect of the whole-word system is not even fully known because many parents pitch in to make it work by teaching phonics at home. A friend of mine sat up many evenings coaching her seven year old from Rudolf Flesch's book *Why Johnny Can't Read and What You Can Do About It*, which presents both a condemnation of the whole-word method and a program of phonic instruction. Judging by the great sale of this book (thirteen months on the best-seller list and still selling well), we might assume that a few hundred thousand other parents also sat up evenings assisting schools with their work. Such home instruction is often carried on secretly by parents not wishing their children to be considered slow learners. But, lo, the achievements of all these teaching parents are counted among the schools' "successes."

THE EDUCATIONAL CON GAME

That a child learns to read in school is not enough. We must ask: What kind of a reader will he become? If a child doesn't read easily and quickly, reading is made less pleasurable for him and is less likely to be indulged. As a result, children who don't read easily tend to read seldom. And those who do not read do not learn. A child's academic career is, therefore, easily jeopardized, and an upper limit is placed upon his learning without the child or his parents ever knowing it has been done.

Reading specialists have a long list of reasons why about one third of all pupils have trouble learning to read. A child will have difficulty, we are told, because his mother doesn't

6. Mary Johnson, *Programmed Illiteracy in Our Schools* (Winnipeg, 1970).

feed him properly. He doesn't get enough sleep. He gets too much sleep. He has no brothers and sisters (is pampered). He has too many brothers and sisters (is confused and neglected). He has no room of his own in which to study. He sees too much television. He is shy. His father drinks. His parents are separated. And so on.

Reading instruction in schools thus becomes like a game of musical chairs in which one third of the players lose their seats even before the music starts. When I read of the nonsense that passes for reading instruction in schools, I thank the day I took a few hours to teach my own children. Now they are safely beyond damage from uncertain, poorly devised reading programs supported by a dishonest educational philosophy.

The danger of entrusting your child to unpredictable school methods is manifest in the popularity of the term *remedial reading*. The phrase has become almost fashionable and has taken on the tone of normalcy, along with inoculations and dental checkups. *Remedial reading* trips off the tongue so easily that one is apt to forget *remedial* means "that which remedies." Why is a remedy for reading necessary? Because many reading programs create problems. What sort of problems? Well, like not being able to read. And so, the three *R*s—reading, 'riting, and 'rithmetic—have been increased to four. Now we have remedial reading.

The most convincing evidence of national decline in reading skill is to be found in the field of mental assessment. In preparing the third edition of the Stanford-Binet IQ test during the mid-1950s, Dr. Maude A. Merrill discovered that the general pattern of children's scores had not changed since the test was last revised in 1937—had not changed, that is, except for one part of the test: reading.

For the reading test, children were required to read a paragraph within thirty-five seconds, recall eight facts in it, and make no more than two errors. Whereas 60 per cent of ten-year-old children had been able to pass this particular test back in 1937, the test now had to be assigned to twelve year olds if the same 60-per-cent pass was to be achieved: unchallengeable proof of a two year decline in national reading ability during a twenty year period.[7]

Ironically, though reading is the subject most poorly taught in schools, it is the one for which the greatest number of tested, proved programs are available. But stranger still, these more efficient programs continue to be used in only 20 per cent of our classrooms.[8]

One hundred seventy-five years ago, Joseph Lancaster taught classes of one thousand children to read in a matter of weeks. Faced with scholastic achievements of this excellence and antiquity, could any modern educationalist seriously assert that the collective efforts of his colleagues and their predecessors had significantly advanced learning during the one-hundred-seventy-five-year period? Surely the record shows the opposite holds true. Educators and educationalists,[9] by ignoring the recommendations of imaginative thinkers, have not merely halted educational advance, they have actually achieved a retrogression. What does all this mean to your child? It means his road to literacy—the common route to all branches of learning—is slippery and treacherous. The chances of your child ever realizing his full scholastic potential are highly uncertain. Educators are waiting to fit your child into their specially designed maze of reading hurdles and hazards. If your child is brilliant, he may learn to read well despite their obstructions. If he *isn't* brilliant, remedial-reading specialists stand ready to assign him a number—another cypher who didn't quite make the grade—and news stories of the following sort may have special bitterness for you in the years ahead: " 'Freshmen going into college today are close to illiterate,' Dr. Benjamin A. Fine,

7. Sybil Terman and Charles C. Walcutt, *Reading: Chaos and Cure* (New York, 1958), p. 15.

8. These programs are listed in the pamphlet *Some Phonetic Systems of Reading*, rev. ed. (Reading Reform Foundation, 1974). (Address on page 207.)

9. Current usage considers *educationalists* to be those who formulate theories of education, which in turn influence teaching techniques in schools and departments of education in colleges and universities—verily, the teaching of teaching. *Educators*, on the other hand, are considered to be professors in the usual curriculum studies: i.e., chemistry, English, history, mathematics and so on.

former education editor of The New York Times . . . told
The Enquirer. 'If we are going to put a stop to the national
disgrace of a third of our college freshmen failing their
courses because they can't read above the sixth-grade level,
there must be a revolutionary change in teaching
method.' " [10]

The remainder of this book presents one possible change.
Let's go back now fourteen months to those preliterate days
so you can see how the girls helped me shape the sixty-day
reading program.

10. *National Enquirer* (January 21, 1973).

PART 2

IMPORTANT: Chapters 5 through 10 describe our program and let you see the sort of problem that may arise while teaching your own child. These chapters should not, however, be thought of as a complete guide for the instruction of your child. Important changes have been made to the program and they are described in Chapters 11 and 12. For example, by teaching the upper-case letters first (instead of last, as I did), you will achieve quicker learning for your child and save yourself much effort.

CHAPTER 5

Leprechauns
in Our Living Room

A puzzle I own shows portions of leprechauns on three pieces of cardboard.[1] When the cards are positioned one way, fourteen Irish dwarfs can be seen. But when the cards are positioned in another way a fifteenth little man suddenly appears. Where does he come from?

The puzzle is just slightly more fascinating to study than the facial expressions of those who attempt to solve it, for, having positioned the pieces all by themselves, the puzzlers then realize they have manipulated an effect that common sense tells them is impossible. Some of the puzzling surprises Eve and Jean provided during our reading lessons seemed no less impossible than the vanishing and reappearing leprechaun, and their surprises began during our very first lesson, Sunday morning, August 27, 1972.

THE 1ST DAY—SUNDAY

With a wide felt-tip pen I printed a 1½ .inch-high letter **a** on the backs of three old business cards, **b** on three others, **c**

1. *The Vanishing Leprechaun* is a modern version of the paradox *Get Off the Earth*, patented in 1896 by the famous American puzzle inventor Sam Loyd.

and **d** on three more each, then announced excitedly I was going to play a game. Would the children care to join in? The girls almost leaped out of their skins in their eagerness to get started.

Children will, of course, readily take up almost any activity if by doing so they secure parental attention. But this is a fickle type of enthusiasm, ever subject to mood, and not to be counted on for a program that might take months to complete. Therefore, Eve and Jean's spontaneous enthusiasm was going to be strengthened—nay, guaranteed—by means of salesmanship, showmanship, and a variety of rewards.

B. F. Skinner's work on operant conditioning proved that rewards can make responses more probable or, in fact, more frequent. Dr. Skinner was able to teach pigeons to walk a figure eight in just five minutes, using a technique called "immediate reinforcement". The birds were given a kernel of corn immediately following any slight movement that contributed to the desired performance. Applying the principle of immediate reinforcement to the education of children, Dr. Skinner developed the first workable teaching machine in 1958—a machine that rewarded pupils by letting them know immediately that their answers were correct, and correctness was itself virtually guaranteed by the skillful way the study matter was presented.

"Correct answer" reward apparently works well with school-age children; but I believed that infants, like pigeons, required a more primitive motivator—something edible. Instead of corn-hungry pigeons, I had raisin-hungry moppets who, at this very moment were eagerly responding to my invitation to play, but with one eye on the box of raisins in my hand.

We don't own a carpet, so I brought the plush, blue bath mat from the bathroom into the living room and sat on it, potentate fashion. The children crowded in expectantly on hands and knees. I had no idea what game we were going to play, but felt certain that almost any repetitive procedure, presented engagingly, would catch the girls' interest.

I showed the girls the letter **a,** told them it stood for a sound, and then sounded the letter for them, not by its name (which sounds like *ay*), but as the letter sounds in *hat*, and, when the children repeated this sound, gave each a raisin. On request, Eve and Jean repeated the sound a few times and received a raisin each time. Did they like this game? Oh, yes.

Then I produced the card for **b** and sounded it, not by its name (which sounds like *bee*), but as it sounds in *tub*.[2] The children repeated the **b** sound three times on request and received a raisin each time. Did they want to continue the game? Yes, indeed. Perhaps they were getting tired? Oh no, no, no!

The cards **a** and **b** were placed side by side and the girls were asked to pronounce one letter, then the other, and so on back and forth. My lavish praise and feigned surprise provided a valuable second form of reward.

Pleased by our quick progress, I showed Eve and Jean a card bearing **c** and sounded the letter, not by its name (which sounds like *see*), but as the letter sounds in *tic*. When the children had sounded **c** a few times, the letters **a, b,** and **c** were placed in a row. To my dismay, the girls now began confusing the letters, and worse, sounded the **b** as a **p**!

I hid my disappointment and even managed to sound enthusiastic, for which the children paid their own reward in the form of affectionate hugs with raisin-sticky fingers. When at last the girls sounded the letters correctly, the card order was changed to **acb**, but again, they became confused, so the cards were quickly changed back to the original **abc** order.

Eve and Jean were still enthusiastic, so we continued with another exercise. I gathered up the cards, now damp with saliva (another hazard), removed the **d**s (there was obviously no hope of the children learning **d**s this first lesson), shuffled the remaining nine cards, then turned them up slowly one at a time for the girls to sound. For all the recognition the children showed, they might have been seeing the letters for the first time. How on earth could Eve and Jean forget what they knew just a moment ago?

Smiling fixedly, I praised the children just for trying, and

2. Precise instructions for correctly duplicating the phonic sounds can be found on page 165.

positioned the cards once again in the formation **abc.** Now they were required to sound the letters from left to right and from right to left for a raisin. Sometimes the girls were able to do this unaided, sometimes not, but in either case, they received a raisin for trying. I halted our first lesson when it had run twenty minutes, and the children went back to their toys.

Later, I attracted their attention to the game again, laid the cards **abc** on the floor, and asked the girls to sound the letters from left to right for a raisin, from right to left for another raisin, then both ways for a third. When Eve and Jean seemed able to recognize the letters easily, another card was added to form the combination **abca,** but errors became so frequent I terminated the session at the end of just ten minutes.

Later in the morning I asked who would like some raisins. Both would, but Jean said she would like the raisins without the game. I gaped with disbelief until she smiled, then advised her that raisins were contingent upon the game. She elected to play, but I soon regretted not having paid more attention to her reluctance. Both children performed badly and the session had to be stopped quickly and cheerfully. I had ignored the fact they were due for a meal and a nap.

When the girls slept, I thought about their performance. How could they know the letters one minute and forget them the next? Why were they able to identify and sound letters in a row, but unable when the letters were presented singly? After mulling this over for a while I began to see that the children hadn't really sounded the letters at all; they had merely sounded the *positions* occupied by the cards—the *left* position was called **a,** the *middle* position was **b,** and the one on the right was **c.** For all the attention Eve and Jean had paid to the shapes of the letters, I might as well have drawn a happy face on each card.

How absurd the shaggy blue bath mat seemed in the living room! Suddenly I saw value in this absurdity. Instead of my suggesting we play the game, the girls should be urging *me* to do so, and the bath mat could work toward that goal. The mat had been placed unobtrusively to one side; now I positioned it prominently in the middle of the floor along with the cards and raisins.

The girls bailed out of their cribs with two loud thumps at 2:30, toddled into the living room scratching and yawning, and unhesitatingly asked to get on with the game. I feigned surprise and indifference, and, while dressing them, voiced weak arguments for not playing the game, but finally acceded on some flimsy condition. Jean had already pried the lid off the plastic container of raisins in her eagerness to get started.

The letter **a** was printed 1½ inches high on a sheet of typing paper and sounded; **b** was printed beneath it and sounded; then **c** was printed beneath **b** and sounded—all done slowly, as if each letter were being shown for the first time. The children's reaction to each was, in fact, as if they *hadn't* seen the letters before. More letters were added, keeping the **a**s on one line, **b**s on another, and **c**s on a third (*Fig. 1*). Despite this segregation, the girls still had great difficulty distinguishing between the letters, and identified **c** three times correctly, only to call it **a** the next time.

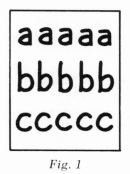

Fig. 1

When, at last, the children recognized the letters easily, the business cards were set out again for them to sound—the row **abc** from left to right (*Fig. 2*). The girls did this with surprising ease, then sounded the letters as easily in the reverse direction. My spirits began to soar. For the final exercise Eve and Jean were required to sound the letters in both directions. When they did this, I almost cheered.

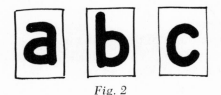

Fig. 2

What an immense relief to see the children master their first three letters! Admittedly, the task had taken longer than I'd expected, but if the girls learned the other letters in the alphabet at even this slow rate, they would soon be reading.

Before proceeding with new letters, it seemed wise to reinforce the children's grasp of the first three; so the nine cards were shuffled and turned up slowly one at a time. Incredibly enough, the girls *still* couldn't recognize the letters! Eve faltered, guessed, and halted; Jean performed no better.

My mind was too confused to cope with the problem, and the strain of pretending to be enthusiastic was draining me, so I ended the session quickly with forced merriment. The girls went back to their toys, and I tried to figure out what was wrong. The answer wasn't long in coming. The children hadn't been identifying *letters*, but instead a top, medium, and bottom row of squiggles.

After a while I went into the girls' room, sat on the floor and, as if it were the most natural topic of conversation in the world, mentioned, in simpler terms, that *all* words had an identifiable sound at their beginning. Eve, busily brushing her doll's hair, pursed her lips but didn't look up. Jean swiveled around on her knees and blinked at me. I interpreted this as encouragement: "Oh, yes. *Apartment* begins with an **a** sound, *box* begins with a **b** sound, and *cat* begins with a **c** sound."

Was I getting through to them? Was my foot in the door? Jean, the younger child, had nodded once, but this didn't necessarily mean anything. I provided a few more examples and asked who could think of a word that began with a **b** sound. Jean suggested *butter*. Hooray! Could anyone think of another word? Silence. I mentioned that some items on the shelves at their elbows began with **b** and **c** sounds, hoping the children might respond with *clock, book,* or one of their toys—*bear, block,* and *car.* But they didn't.

Trying a different approach, I said I'd draw something that began with a **c** sound, and drew a cat. Could they think of something for me to draw that began with the **a, b,** or **c** sound? They couldn't.

I opened a book containing games of recognition, and slowly turned the pages. Could they see anything that started with the **a, b,** or **c** sound? Eve suggested *nurse,* Jean suggested *train.* I patted their heads, left them, and wondered whether the reading program was really such a good idea after all.

After baths, I asked who would like some raisins. The children responded by suggesting we play the game. Here at least was a good sign. Raisins and reading were now a "packaged deal" in their minds. They had accepted the reading sessions as a pleasant eating program with minor interruptions between treats.

I printed **a** 1½ inches high with a thick felt-tip pen. Eve and Jean weren't able to identify the letter, so *I* sounded it and paid them a raisin for correctly repeating the sound. When they had repeated the sound a few times, for another raisin each time, I printed **b**. Again, the girls couldn't recall the sound, so we repeated the procedure used for **a**. Then I printed **c** and the children confounded me by sounding it correctly! When, once again, Eve and Jean seemed able to distinguish between the first three letters, we reviewed all the earlier exercises with the business cards.

Jean improved during this twenty-minute exercise, Eve regressed. Indeed, she made so many mistakes both children burst out laughing. I managed a strained smile.

We had spent a total of one hour twenty minutes on reading this first day. So little progress for so much effort suddenly made the task of teaching the girls seem infinitely more difficult than I had imagined it might be. But nothing if not optimistic, I began considering the best order in which to present the other letters of the alphabet, weighing which letters might be confused with the first three—either because of sound or appearance—and which letters permitted the greatest number of words to be constructed.

THE 2ND DAY

The reading sessions on Sunday had provided a welcome change from the children's squabbling, shrieking, nonsense singing, giggling, banging into things, and howling over nothing. Weekdays were another matter. The girls spent each day at a nursery, and its administrators asked that children arrive no later than 9:00 A.M. Consequently, our departure each morning was sometimes frenzied.

You perhaps already know that children of two and three are equipped with five thumbs on each hand, four of which don't change into fingers until about age four. Despite the task of getting the children washed, dressed, fed, wiped, buttoned, combed, zippered, tied, and pointed in the right direction each morning, I was determined that they would have a reading lesson, however brief.

I set aside fourteen raisins and, finding two eager takers, began the exercise. The a, b, and c cards were positioned in that order on the floor. The children couldn't identify a but remembered b and c. Indisputable progress!

The girls sounded the sequence in one direction, then in the other, and finally in both directions. Six raisins paid. Next, the cards were placed in the sequence bac, and the procedure was repeated. Errors occurred and prompting was necessary, but, encouragingly, the girls rarely repeated their errors. Twelve raisins gone. The last two raisins went quickly, and so did we—down the long hall to the elevator.

We saw a bus while driving to the nursery. What sound does the word *bus* begin with? Even though I sounded the b with great exaggeration, the girls couldn't isolate the beginning sound, nor could they do so for other items—*barn, cow, car,* and so on. But when asked to supply a word starting with a b sound, Jean said *bread.* Good!

The girls were fed hearty noon meals at the nursery and four-o'clock snacks too, so good appetites at suppertime were not always certain. If the reading session *followed* supper each day the raisins might not have enough motivating power, and if the session *preceeded* supper, then the raisins would lessen the children's appetite still more. Believing that Eve and Jean wouldn't be dwarfed or seriously misshapen by having light suppers for a while, I gave the reading program priority.

While the vegetables cooked, I asked who would like some raisins and, receiving enthusiastic responses, printed the letter **a** on a piece of paper. Jean remembered the sound; Eve didn't, and though neither child remembered **b**, both sounded **c**.

The children took turns sounding **abc** forward then in the reverse order for the second exercise, and, finally, both ways in a single turn. When each child had performed the exercises three times, the entire procedure was repeated for letter combinations **bac, bca,** and **abca**. The session lasted fifteen minutes.

After supper (which Eve alone ate), we visited a shopping plaza. While driving, I quizzed the children on the beginning sounds of various words. The sounds were accentuated by stuttering: "Who knows what sound *b-b-b-building* starts with?" The same question was posed for *bus, bear, apple, car,* and others in a singsong manner to make a game of it, and the girls answered several queries correctly.

The children were mustered for still another session between bathtime and brushing teeth. I pointed out, regretfully, that we could play for only a few minutes and that there were but ten raisins. The girls almost knocked me over in their eagerness to tap the dwindling supply. Apparently, limited quantity and limited availability rouse raisin-hungry children as readily as bargain-hungry shoppers.

The letter **a** was printed 1½ inches high on a piece of paper. Could anyone sound the letter? To my surprise, the children gave, in one voice, the correct response. More, they did the same for **b** and **c**! Then, using the cards, we practiced just the more difficult exercises from the earlier session (sounding the combinations **bac, bca,** and **abca** both ways).

Toward the end of the lesson I intensified the children's

interest by announcing: "There are only *five* raisins left . . . *four* raisins . . ." and so on. Indeed, enthusiasm was so high when the raisins were gone that I felt obliged to produce six more in the name of "special bonus;" but I did it with the sober reminder that these six were absolutely the last for the evening. The children nodded understandingly.

I might as well have saved the high-powered motivating techniques for another time because Eve, though enthusiastic, performed badly. Doubtless, the children were highly motivated to play, but the game itself was ineffectual; it simply wasn't making the information lodge in their minds.

A solution of sorts lay in increased exposure of the letters, so when the children were in bed I printed **a, b,** and **c** 10 inches high in strokes 1 inch thick on large cards and tacked them to the ceiling between the girls' cribs. Three smaller letters were attached to the apartment door for the children's perusal while they awaited our departure each morning.

The bath mat, now damp from its proper function, was returned to the living room. Cards and raisins prominently displayed around the mat suggested a miniature market place of learning. Indeed, with letters now on the floor, the wall, and the ceiling, the whole apartment was beginning to look like a bazaar. In my self-cast role of educational merchant, I looked forward to brisk, profitable trade on the morrow.

But I didn't allow for pinworms.

CHAPTER 6

Triumph with
the First Sentences

THE 3RD DAY

Pinworms, it seems, lay eggs so tiny they can be borne by air currents and inhaled. But after supplying this interesting (if awkward) conversational nugget, my encyclopedia gave no hint for the expulsion of the parasites. What to do? The only worms I'd ever dealt with were the type that fit onto hooks.

Assuming that Eve and Jean's condition would make them unwelcome at the nursery, I phoned. The director waved aside the children's infestation as if it were nothing more than the hiccups, suggested I pick up some medicine and bring the girls in as usual.

The children's spirits were apparently unaffected, for Jean had awakened me by shaking the raisin container like a rhythm instrument, urging me to play. I collected my thoughts, sat on the mat, and printed a large **a** which the girls promptly named **b**; however, they identified **b** and **c** correctly.

Removing ten raisins from the container, I stressed the limited number and limited time for playing and presented the sequences **bac, cab,** and **acb.** When these raisins were gone, I rewarded the girls by producing another six, then relented yet again later and withdrew another four from the box, followed by an additional two, all of which permitted each child thirteen turns. Jean made no errors, but Eve made several.

Dressed, fed, and ready to leave, the children sounded the letters on the hall door while waiting for me to find the car keys.

The girls seemed no worse for their worms at five o'clock, so we followed the procedure of the night before—one session as soon as we arrived home, followed by bath, supper, then another session just before teeth brushing.

The children sounded the sequences **bac, cab,** and **acb** three times each in both directions. Errors were greeted with a hearty and encouraging "Nearly!" and the girls were urged to try again. Jean made mistakes on two attempts, Eve on four.

When the weather was nice, Eve and Jean spent much of the day playing in the nursery yard, so they were often stained, smudged, if not caked, with dirt by five o'clock. Therefore, baths usually took priority over food, and while they splashed in the tub, I prepared supper. Today I risked periodic splashing to show the girls a card bearing the letter **s,** sounding it not by the name of the letter (which sounds like *ess*), but by making a hissing sound.

By learning **s,** the children would be able to read their first word, *scab.* But they didn't yet know what a scab was, so I pointed to one on Eve's leg. Jean lost no time in hunting up a small scratch on her own leg. Technically, the girls could have read *cab* at this point, but they didn't know that cab was another word for taxi. (I made a mental note to tell them in traffic tomorrow.)

The one-shot treatment for pinworms was to follow a meal, so after supper each child received a teaspoonful of strawberry-flavored medicine in the name of "special treat." Dosage went by body weight—I drank six teaspoonsful. Prost! Now, who would like some raisins? Jean responded with a flat "No,"—she wanted cornflakes. Taking this to mean she didn't want to play the game, I let the matter drop. Later, with greater exuberance, I offered raisins again, but Jean still wanted cornflakes. Did the child perhaps mean she wanted individual cornflakes as reading rewards? Assuming this, but not daring to ask, I poured out a bowlful of cornflakes, and we quickly ran through the exercises. Jean made no errors; her older sister made three. The letter s was shown and sounded separately a few times, then added to the game in the sequences **sacb** and **scab,** which the girls successfully sounded in both directions.

The time had now arrived for the children to read their first word, and I announced this fact in a tone and manner befitting a grand occasion. The children watched, spellbound, as I slowly (for effect) drew the cards close together to form the word **scab.** I began sounding each letter, slowly at first, then repeated the sequence of sounds over and over again with increasing speed. Finally, to link the letters together physically, I printed **scab** in 1¾-inch characters on a piece of paper.

I'm not sure what reaction I expected from the children, and to this day, I'm still not sure what their expressions conveyed. They seemed to know that something important had happened, if only by the delighted expression on father's face. In any case, the girls provided the final surprise by picking up the individual letters and placing them atop the appropriate letters of the printed word.

THE 4TH DAY

With all the pinworms now dead or extremely ill, I could concentrate on the problems of reading. Jean was no sooner out of bed, than she began badgering me to play the game. I expressed mock surprise and mock reluctance (anything I'm reluctant to do, the children want to do all the more), then finally agreed to play for a couple of minutes. Having overslept, we were, in fact, rushed. The children sounded the combinations **bac, cab, acb, sacb, scab** twice each, repeating any group in which an error occurred. Jean made one mistake, Eve *seventeen.*

While shopping with the children late this afternoon I named various things we saw, exaggerating the beginning sound of each. The word *cab* was reinforced whenever a taxi appeared: "Look, there's a cab. What is it? That's right, a cab. Who'll see the next cab first?"

After baths, Jean suggested we play the game. Thinking cornflakes less upsetting to their appetites than raisins, I offered cornflakes. Taken! The girls were to sound the combinations **bac** twice for a payoff each try, then do the same with **bca.** Jean managed this easily, but Eve required ten tries.

Bored by waiting for her sister, Jean didn't want to play any more. Perhaps she could be lured back to the exercises by a new game. No! Even without seeing it, Jean didn't want to play. Not to be put off so easily, I began the new game with Eve, and counted on the fascinating procedure to catch Jean's fancy.

Three red blocks of wood (from a set of building blocks) 1 inch by 2 inches by 3½ inches, were positioned a few inches apart on their ends, their widths facing Eve. A card bearing the word **scab** was affixed to the top of one block, **cab** to another, and **bac** to a third (*Fig. 3*).

Fig. 3. A word block.

For phonic simplicity, minor spelling errors were to be incorporated in our program at first, so **bac** was to represent **back.** My decision to include small inaccuracies was influenced by i.t.a., the forty-four-character Initial Teaching Alphabet which employs "calculated errors" to simplify reading.

doun ʃhe strɛɛt cæm ʃhe mælman.

"lemonæd, lemonæd, fiev sents a glass!" cried ʃhe ʧhildren.

"well," sed ʃhe mælman. "ʃhat's a gɷd iedea on a dæ liek ʃhis. ie'll hav a glass."

polly stirrd. molly pord.

Fig. 4

After learning to read by this completely phonetic method, a gradual change is made to traditional letter forms and spelling. Children taught reading by the i.t.a. method apparently become good readers despite the adjustments they must ultimately make. It seemed unlikely, therefore, that Eve and Jean would be greatly confused later to learn that **bac** was missing a **k**. And so, there were now three common words that the girls were technically capable of reading: **cab, scab, bac.**

The new game consisted of trying to knock over one of the three word-blocks by rolling a toy car. When successful, Eve sounded the combination of letters on that block, from left to right only, then spoke the complete word. Soon Jean wanted to play too, and they had a great time careening the car across the floor.

For me, the game was a waste of time. Under the children's clumsy guidance, the car often swerved away and missed the blocks. Eve had great difficulty identifying the letters, and neither child was able to relate the sounds of the letters to the sounds of the words the letters formed. After sounding the individual letters in **cab**, for example, the girls invariably read it as **scab**.

THE 5TH DAY

Jean didn't want to join in the session this morning but soon changed her mind at the sight and sound of Eve munching her first rewards. I had decided we would no longer employ meaningless letter combinations. All sequences would now have to form words. Furthermore, the children would sound the letters only in a normal left-to-right manner, no longer the reverse. But we needed more words to work with, so the girls were shown the letter **u** occasionally, sounded not by its name (which sounds like *you*) but by the sound it represents in *nut*. The entire session was kept short—less than five minutes—to generate enthusiasm for the more important lessons later in the day.

Before supper, the building blocks were positioned as before, but the children were to roll a marble instead of the toy car. This solved the problem of swerving, but, alas, the marble wasn't heavy enough to topple, or even disturb, the blocks. I quickly printed **cab, scab,** and **bac** on three small pieces of paper, snipped two vertical slits on their bottom edges, bent the three sections outward to form "feet," and substituted the stand-up papers for the blocks (*Fig. 5*).

Fig. 5

Now we were all set to go. But the children's interest had waned during the moments of production and they didn't want to play. I changed the reward from raisins to cheese-flavored corn-puff sticks (which we simply called "cheesies"), and the game was immediately under way.

The paper targets were positioned far enough apart to insure occasional misses, but because the children had *two* marbles to roll each turn, they seldom missed with both rolls.

Some of the cheese puffs were 3 and 4 inches long, and, even though composed mostly of air, they lessened the children's appetites for supper, so I established the rule that three targets had to be hit for a single payoff. Hits were recorded by giving the children a tiddlywink each time.

The results were depressing. Much time was spent retrieving marbles from various parts of the room. This plus occasional misses and time for the children to sound the letters and words—which they frequently did wrong—permitted little learning to take place.

The letter **u** was shown occasionally and sounded. The girls appeared to gain little by hearing that *umbrella* began with the **u** sound; perhaps because, by their pronunciation of it, *umbrella* and *ambrella* are indistinguishable.

The game was put aside and the children simply took turns sounding letters and words. Though the same errors in identification persisted, there was now at least more frequent opportunity for instruction and correction. Nevertheless, I had to bring the session to an early halt because my patience seemed to be running out. Indeed, I noted a slightly hysterical quality in my voice.

THE 6TH DAY

To rouse enthusiasm for the games this morning, I had covered the bath mat last night with a dazzling array of learning hardware—the three red building blocks with the cards **bac, scab,** and **cab** still affixed; the paper targets for the marble game; the marbles; six colored tiddlywinks; a sheet of paper with **cab, scab,** and **bac** printed in even larger letters; the container of raisins; an immense bag of cheese puffs; and a bowl of cornflakes. Then I had removed any object near the mat that might distract from the visual feast.

Ooh! Aah!

Feigning surprise at the children's interest, I let myself be swayed into conducting a short session. The girls sounded the letters **bac,** read the word, then did the same for **scab** and

cab. The letter **u** was shown periodically, and, in preparation for its use in the exercise, I explained that a cub was a baby bear. By then it was breakfast time.

Between mouthfuls, Jean stressed her desire to return to the game after breakfast. Fine, but she had to eat half an orange first. And she did, but Eve balked. I reduced the situation to simple terms—no orange, no game. From my position, this was a no-loss choice. If Eve ate the orange and joined us, good; if she didn't eat the orange, she would see that the reading session was a privilege that would be withheld for obstinacy. This gave me another bargaining tool while elevating the children's estimation of the game.

To add enticement, I began playing the most flamboyant game (the car and blocks) with Jean. The orange disappeared and Eve joined us, wearing an I-ate-it-you-tyrant expression. But as soon as the children had each taken a couple of turns, they were maneuvered from the inefficient car-and-blocks game to the highly repetitive, if less appealing, pastime of simply sounding letters and words.

Eve's performance was no better than before breakfast. She sounded the letters **bac** correctly, but then sounded the combination **cab** as if it were **bac** too. How on earth could she be 100-per-cent right one instant and 100-per-cent wrong the next? The children would have to be exposed to the first three words more frequently.

I found time during the day to print **scab** on six variously sized slips of purple paper, **cab** on six yellow slips, and **bac** on six blue ones. The first set of one purple, one yellow, and one blue slip were then snipped and bent for the marble game, and a second set of three slips was affixed to blocks for the car game. (Even though we probably wouldn't use these two games again, the equipment necessary for their play added color to the bath mat.) A third set of slips was for actual use in our exercises, and a fourth set was destined for the hall door. The fifth set was for the ceiling over the children's cribs, and the sixth for the ceiling in my bedroom/living room/studio. (To avoid whispering and giggling after the light was out, one child slept in my bed until either she or her sister was asleep.)

When the children marched in from the nursery this afternoon and saw the blaze of color on the bath mat, they couldn't wait to get started; and after baths, they sounded the letters and read the three words four times—requiring each of them to identify forty letters.

Cheesies were now substituted for raisins. Enthusiasm rocketed and the children sped on through another five turns. I then stopped the game—over their protests—for they had interpreted and sounded ninety letters and thirty words each.

The use of different colored paper for each word may have aided word recognition, though this was neither intended nor desired. However, Eve's occasional confusion between **cab** and **bac** seemed to indicate little reliance on color.

THE 7TH DAY—SATURDAY

Before beginning a three-hour drive to spend the long holiday week end with friends near Lake Ontario, Eve and Jean were induced to sound **cab, scab,** and **bac** four times each. After the drive, in different surroundings, the children repeated the same exercise five times with only one error between them. Great! They had little difficulty with two new words—**us** (three soundings, one error) and **bus** (two soundings, no errors).

Could this improved performance be due to the new method of payment? During the first few sessions of our program the children had often seemed to err, not so much because they didn't know the answer, but simply because they were half-thinking of something else. The progressive form of payment today may have helped to concentrate their attention on the task. The ascending order of gustatory delights was:

> first sounding of three words = 1 raisin
> second sounding of three words = 2 raisins
> third sounding of three words = 3 raisins
> fourth sounding of three words = ½ of a long cheesie
> subsequent soundings = ½ of a long cheesie

The seven-o'clock session went well—just four errors in nineteen soundings of **cab, scab,** and **bac** and no errors in a single sounding of **us** and **bus.**

THE 8TH DAY—SUNDAY

Being away from my own work area and free of household chores—on a real holiday, in fact—permitted me to give more time to the children. We had three long sessions of about forty minutes each today. The children's enthusiasm ran high, and they each sounded a total of 125 words. Eve occasionally confused **cab** and **bac**. But, strangely, my star performer, Jean, began confusing **cab** and **scab**. She sounded the letters correctly for **scab**, then read the complete word as **cab**. I gently corrected her, but she immediately, repeated the error. In fact, out of fourteen attempts, Jean was correct only four times! A friend, watching from across the room, shook his head in disbelief, unable to understand how the error could persist despite repeated correction. But the more baffling part lay in the fact that before becoming confused Jean had sounded these same letters and read the word correctly twenty-five times!

THE 9TH DAY—LABOR DAY, MONDAY

The children have developed an odd manner of dealing with each word. They sound the individual letters, then cup their hands around their mouths, swallow hard, and whisper the word. This strange ritual seemed particularly effective today, for the girls were correct most of the time. I waited until Jean's confidence was brimming then had her try **scab**. Out of seven tries, she was correct four times.

After a 150-mile drive home, we had our only other session of the day while supper cooked. Hoping to form a stronger link in the children's minds between the letter sounds and the word sounds, I made an identical set of word strips on identically colored paper—**cab** on yellow, **scab** on purple, **bac** on blue, **bus** on red, and **us** on pale green—then cut the words apart, letter by letter. To sound a word now, the children had to position each letter in the correct order, sound the letters individually, then read the word.

Distressingly, the children positioned the letters in the wrong order, sounded them correctly (in that wrong order), then sounded the words as if the letters were in the *right* order! When they had failed with **cab** and **bus,** the girls tried the simplest word of all, **us,** and they succeeded in aligning and identifying the letters twice each (though Jean cared little if the **u** was upside down). The exercise, requiring as it did the children's manipulation of the lettered pieces, couldn't have proceeded more slowly had the girls been wearing boxing gloves. But there seemed no other way to let them see how chains of individual letters formed recognizable words.

Next, the girls aligned **cab** and **bus.** Eve's performance was error-free in fifteen tries, but Jean made six errors in fourteen attempts to align **scab,** which she persists in calling **cab.** There *must* be a logical reason for her reading **scab** as **cab.** Children don't make mistakes without good reason.

THE 10TH DAY

We repeated last night's exercise at 7:45 this morning. To help the children align the letters correctly, a specimen of each word printed in large letters on its appropriately colored paper was placed in front of them for reference. The alignment and sounding went well, though the girls showed little concern for placing the letters right side up. But here was pure logic: a chair remains a chair whether its feet are on the floor or pointing toward the ceiling. Why shouldn't the same apply to letters of the alphabet? The children were shown the preferred way of positioning each letter, then we turned to breakfast. Jean wanted to play again after breakfast, but we didn't have time.

The children placed the letters right side up more frequently at our 5:45 session. Jean continued to sound **scab** as **cab** every three or four times, and my face was beginning to hurt from looking pleased. I chided her gently about the recurring error and, thinking she was tired, suggested we stop. She insisted on continuing.

To provide a change, the word **cub** was introduced. Jean immediately sounded the **b** as an **s,** and having made the error once, repeated it every few tries. The word **suc** (for *suck*) was then introduced, and each child sounded first the letters then the word without mistake.

During our final session after supper, Jean's confusion of **scab** and **cab** reached the point where she had almost interchanged the identity of the words. I laughed and tried to end the session. She insisted on continuing, but her performance didn't improve. The words **cab** and **scab** were becoming a hindrance to learning; more was to be gained by proceeding with new material, so **t** was printed on a card and sounded several times (not as *tee*, but as the sound at the end of *net*).

Jean's manner today was as puzzling as her performance, for, throughout the exercises, she insisted she was a cow, so I was obliged to say, "All right, Cow, now please have another try at this."

THE 11TH DAY

Jean urged me three times to begin the prebreakfast game. Once started, the children positioned letters to form **bac, us, bus, cub, suc,** and sounded the letters and words three times. **Scab** and **cab** were included in Eve's exercises, but not in Jean's. Between them, the girls sounded 121 letters and 42 words. The only error during the entire session occurred when Jean inadvertently positioned a **b** upside down in **bac.**

Neither child seemed in the mood for games at 5:30, so the session was quickly ended. Just before bedtime, I asked if anyone would care for cheesies and was almost bowled over by the response. Watching the girls perform at a new peak of enthusiasm made me realize that the imminence of bed was a powerful teaching aid. Even my mock surprise at the children's continued interest was hardly needed to ensure their best performance yet.

Eve sounded **cab** and **scab** twice. Individual letters and specimens of the words **cat** and **tub** were introduced, and the children formed and sounded these several times. Between them Even and Jean sounded a total of 322 letters and 112 words—all without a single error!

Eve has developed a new ritual for processing words. She sounds the component letters, then says "Now that's . . . ," takes a deep breath, and reads the word aloud. The words "Now that's" plus the breath give her an extra two or three seconds to reconsider her interpretation of the word.

Out of curiosity, I showed Jean the word **cab.** She looked away and appeared too busy with other matters to respond.

THE 12TH DAY

When the bag containing the cheese puffs had split a few days ago, the contents had been transferred to a plastic bread wrapper—a poor choice because the printed pattern and lettering obscured the mouth-watering contents. Now, with that bagful eaten, an immense new, clear plastic container of puffs was set out as bait.

On awaking, Jean promptly asked to begin the game. The link between the letter sounds and the word sounds was now secure enough in the children's minds to dispense with the time-consuming manipulation of individual letters, so only the 2½-inch-by-6-inch slips of paper bearing the specimen words were set out. The girls sounded the letters, read the complete words **bus, cub, suc, cat,** and **tub** five times each, then practiced a new word, **but,** twice—all without error!

The children were in a silly mood this afternoon, so I stopped the proceedings despite their protests. During the 8:30 session they worked diligently with **us, bus, suc, cat,** and **cub;** then **tub** and **but** were added. Altogether, Eve read 101 words with only one error; Jean read the same number, and, in addition, periodically read **bac** for a total seventeen times (no errors) and **scab** thirty-one times (four errors).

Each time Jean was shown **scab,** she would say, "I don't want to do that one," to which I would reply, "You mean you don't want to do **scab?**" Furnished thus with the correct pronunciation, she would respond, "Oh, all right," and quickly sound the word before she forgot it.

The children's enthusiasm was maintained in three ways during this forty-five-minute session. First, the payoff was attractive: for sounding nine words each turn the girls received two long cheese puffs. Then, after fifteen minutes of exercises, my feigned astonishment and tomfoolery prompted them to play another fifteen minutes. Thereafter, I had only to glance at my watch and express concern about bedtime to propel them on for another fifteen minutes. Indeed, the girls were more alert and eager at the end of the session than they were at the start (witness, Eve complained bitterly because I had stopped the session "just before" her turn!).

THE 13TH DAY

I lengthened this morning's session because an art assignment would prevent our having lessons later in the day. The children began with four words. Others were gradually added to make eight. Each child sounded the individual and combined letters of forty-five words.

Jean, again in her role of cow, sounded the letters in a high-pitched, ullulating manner, but whenever she experienced difficulty, she quickly changed to her normal voice. The word **scab** was placed before her periodically, with the assertion, "You can sound **scab** all right now, can't you, Cow?" And, of course, she could.

THE 14TH DAY—SATURDAY

During our two sessions today, the children easily learned a new word, **cut.** Jean's difficulty with **scab** seemed to be over, but she still looked away when shown **cab.**

For some reason, the girls sounded each letter loudly and jabbed their fingers onto the appropriate letter of the words with a force that almost penetrated the slips lying on the fluffy bathmat. The children showed better distinction in their pronunciation of **a** and **u.**

THE 15TH DAY—SUNDAY

We were out most of the day so no sessions were possible. This evening, the children were shown **ee** a couple of times and words containing **ee—see, meet,** and **beet** (*beetroot*).

THE 16TH DAY

Seeming listless this morning, Eve couldn't pronounce **see** and **beet,** and didn't want to try. Jean, however, did so without difficulty ten times, then went on to read **suc, cat,** and **scab.** Pleased with her mastery of **scab,** Jean asked for the **cab** slip, and when I found it, she sounded the letters and read the word correctly. But on her next reading of **scab,** she fell back into her old habit of reading it as **cab.** I hid the **cab** slip once again and vowed to leave it hidden.

This afternoon, as soon as the children were in the car they were shown the letter **m,** and heard it, not by its name (which sounds like *em*) but as a humming sound. While driving home, I pointed to and named items that began with the **m** sound.

After baths, Jean sounded the letters, then the words **meet, mat, beet,** and **see** easily, but Eve balked at the three words containing **ee.** In a rash move, I offered her three cheesies to sound the components of those three words, and she did— three times each!

A short session just before bedtime would strengthen Eve's grasp of **ee.** I asked: Who would like cheesies? No one. Who would like grapes? No one. All right, anyone for potato chips? We were in business. But it soon became obvious that Eve was genuinely tired, so we played for just a couple of minutes.

THE 17TH DAY

Jean had diarrhea, Eve had a runny nose, but the girls were enthusiastic for their morning session. Each child sounded **meet, mat, beet,** and **see** four times, then the ten "old" words once: **scab, bus, us, cub, cat, but, cut, bac, suc,** and **tub.** Eve had no difficulty with **ee.** Finally, the girls were shown two new words, **I** and **you. You,** being phonically irregular, was taught as a whole word, with no regard to its individual letters.

Shopping prevented our having a presupper lesson this afternoon, so I hoped the later session might compensate for the loss. And it did. In fact, the results exceeded my greatest expectation.

The children began by reading the words **meet, mat, beet, see,** and occasionally **I** and **you,** followed by a rerun of the ten "old" words. Ordinarily, the session would have ended there, but during her last sounding of **meet, mat, beet,** and **see,** Jean didn't trouble to sound the letters at all—she simply read the complete words. Wondering whether she might be ready to read her first sentence, I positioned the three slips **I, see, you** in that order and asked her to read them. She did so without hesitation and, realizing *what* she had done, looked up in surprise. I quickly added another slip bearing **Eve** (a word already known by sight to both children). Laughing delightedly, Jean read, **I see you Eve.**

When Eve realized what was happening, that a chain of familiar symbols was making sense, she couldn't push her little sister out of the way fast enough to have a try.

Grasping the moment, I printed **a** on a card, introduced it as a new word, and arranged the word strips to form **I see a cat.** Then, together, we slowly read the sentence, though I made sure my voice lagged behind theirs or, if it had to precede theirs, sounded no more than the first letter.

The word **beet** replaced **cat,** and the girls slowly read **I see a beet.** The children's excitement was mounting now. They impatiently shouldered one another aside for a turn as each new sentence was formed: **I see a mat. I see a bus, I see a scab.** Then **you** replaced **I** to form: **you see a bus, you see a cat, you see a scab.** Finally, I composed the sentence **you meet a cat,** but the children were now growing tired (and considering their poor health, this wasn't surprising).

I stepped onto the balcony when the children were asleep, leaned contentedly on the railing, and gazed off at the immense clock in the Peace Tower on Parliament Hill, a small white dot low in the sky three miles away. The children were indisputably reading, lifting meaningful thoughts from sound symbols. My task now was simply to add new letters at an unhurried pace, slowly enough that the children wouldn't feel anxious or uncertain.

CHAPTER 7

The Automobile as
a Vehicle for Learning

Our learning-to-read campaign seems ever destined to progress in a rhythmic series of advances and retreats. We advance in an oddly choreographed march of two steps forward, one step back. Two thirds of our tiny combat force reported sick this morning, suffering one or more symptoms of flu. But morale was high, so we mustered for an assault on the printed word.

The first setback occurred when Eve developed a conceptual blank spot for **you,** and, in fact, had to be shown the word a dozen times before she could remember it. Even *she* had to smile over her puzzling forgetfulness. (When, out of curiosity, I quizzed her ten minutes after the session ended, she had forgotten the word again!)

A more mystifying quirk—the children began reading words that weren't there. First one child, then the other read **I see you** as **I see** *a* **you.** Many attempts and much coaching were required before the girls finally omitted the nonexistent **a.** But now they really began loosing the leprechauns.

The colored slips were positioned to form **I see a cat,** and when the children read the sentence correctly, the word **tub** was substituted for **cat.** Now, Jean began reading **see** as if it

95

had no **s**. Appalled, I asked Eve to read the sentence, but, as if by some supernatural contagion, she couldn't sound the **s** in **see** either. Much coaching was required before the girls could again read **see** correctly.

Our sole gain for the morning—the children learned **wee** (for *we*). This spelling was used so the girls wouldn't be confused by seeing the single **e** in **we** sounded the same as the double **e** in **see, beet,** and **meet.**

While driving to the nursery, I repeatedly flashed the word **you** for Eve, but at the nursery door she still couldn't remember it. Nor could she identify **you** this afternoon. Worse, after being told the word, she couldn't remember it for even three minutes. As soon as we reached the apartment I drew a happy face inside the **o** of **you,** and, tapping her head gently, said "That's *you?*" Consequently, Eve was able to recall the word not just ten minutes later, but two hours later.

A splinter in Eve's foot required much delicate probing, and this shortened our presupper session. Eve read **you** easily, but still insisted on inserting **a** before it.

Jean, not a complainer by nature, winced because of her sore throat. I had the same affliction and knew it was painful. She reacted to the discomfort with affectionate aggression and, while waiting her turn, climbed onto my back and hung over my shoulder.

Following her bath, Eve was moody and wouldn't participate, but Jean, despite her sore throat, read sentences composed of **I, you,** and **we,** the verbs **see** and **meet,** the nouns **bus, beet, mat,** and so on. The sentences, composed as they were of variously colored word slips, resembled a train of railway cars, so we dubbed them "word trains" (*Fig. 6*).

Fig. 6. A word train.

THE 19TH DAY

When the morning session began, at Jean's urging, the children were shown how, by using an s printed on a small slip of paper, the words on the slips could be made plural. Happily, the girls accepted and remembered this information easily. I learned something too—the sound of s is determined by the word it is added to. For example, when added to **tub, s** is buzzed; but it is hissed when added to **cat.** Rather than expose the children to the arbitrary sounding of this letter, s wasn't added to **tub, see, cab, cub,** and **scab.**

The word train **I see you Eve** was composed, and when each child had read it, cars in the train were changed to form new sentences. In this way, the following six sentences were read.

A-1.	**I see you Eve**	**A-4.**	**you see cats**
A-2.	**I see a mat**	**A-5.**	**you see a bus**
A-3.	**I see beets**	**A-6.**	**wee see a cub**

(The letter A preceding each sentence serves only to distinguish this group of sentences—the A group—from sentence groups B, C, D, E, and F that will ultimately be introduced.)

Because Jean was first to read each new sentence formed, Eve gained an advantage in word identification. Despite this, she faltered on the very first sentence, and this prompted young Jean to coach her in what struck me as being a most considerate manner. Eve also had difficulty with the sixth sentence, but spurned any attempt to end the session; and, after several more failures, she read sentence A-6 correctly.

The letter f was shown and sounded (not as *eff*, but as the sound at the end of *cuff*). On the way to the nursery, I asked what familiar words began with that sound, hoping the girls might respond with **face, feet, far,** or **Fatty** (Jean's nickname), but they couldn't think of a thing. Later in the day, on the drive home, the children were again invited to suggest words that began with **f.** They enjoyed the game immensely, but unfortunately, contributed nothing to it.

Once home, I announced excitedly that they would now meet two new words. This revelation, made in a manner appropriate to the presentation of a great gift, engaged the children's rapt attention. Slips bearing **fat** and **feet** were laid out. To my surprise, Eve took the lead in decoding [1] the new words. The word trains formed during the session were:

A-7.	you see a scab	A-10.	wee see a fat cat
A-8.	I see feet	A-11.	I see a fat cub
A-9.	wee see a tub		

The exercise was repeated briefly just before bedtime and went well, though Eve had forgotten **you** again. To end, the children read the twenty-one words they now knew.

THE 20TH DAY

Only two sessions were possible today, and both were spent reviewing sentences A-1 to A-11. During the second lesson, the girls were shown the letter **i** (sounded not as *eye,* but as in *if*). This news was greeted with considerable indifference.

THE 21ST DAY—SATURDAY

The girls were shown the letter **i** again, then two new words, **sic** (*sick*) and **biscit** (*biscuit*). Suddenly realizing the children didn't know **am,** I quickly introduced it, then formed two new trains:

A-12.   I am sic   A-13.   I see biscits

Eve and Jean read the two new sentences, then A-1 to A-11 three times each before going back to their toys (the girls didn't attend nursery on Saturdays).

Strips of variously colored paper, 2½ inches by 10 inches, were cut, and sentences A-1 to A-13 were printed on them in 1-inch letters, two sentences on each strip, one per side (*Fig.* 7). The strips would yield three benefits. First, all words in each sentence would now be on the same color paper, so color could no longer provide a clue to the identity of indi-

---

1. Sounding individual letters in order to read a word.

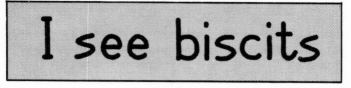

Fig. 7. A sentence strip.

vidual words. Second, the reduced size of print (half the previous size) would be a big step toward reading normal book print. Third, time would no longer be wasted in searching for and positioning individual word slips and in adding an s where needed.

With fitting ceremony, the new strips were set before the children this afternoon. I am sorry to report, however, that the sentences might as well have been printed in Japanese. Even Jean began guessing over the simplest words. After failing twice to get the session rolling I went back to composing word trains, and, as the girls read them, pointed out the similarity of each word in the train to its counterpart on the sentence strip.

After supper, Jean complained of a sore throat, but I suspected her greater problem was tiredness—she hadn't slept at nap time. Anyway, she didn't want to play the game, nor did she want Eve collecting rewards without her. Of course, no greater incentive was possible for Eve to deliver a spectacular reading performance, and, after reading two word trains, she put aside the word slips and read solely from the sentence strips. Not to be left out altogether, Jean read a couple of sentence strips, though to do so, she had to keep referring to the word slips now discarded in a central heap. Why was she so dependent on the word slips? Did the different-sized letters confuse her, or had the different colored papers previously provided a clue? Perhaps both.

When the children were tucked in bed I announced excitedly that tomorrow they would be shown a new word—**my.** This drew "Ohs" of wonder.

THE 22ND DAY—SUNDAY

Much more than the introduction of **my** was needed to raise Jean's spirits this morning. Her throat was still sore, and she performed poorly, missed easy words, guessed, and even hid sentence strips in an attempt to end the session. Eve read all the sentences easily.

The six-o'clock session proceeded at a dreadfully slow rate. Jean kept insisting she had never seen some of the words before, so I was obliged to find the appropriate word slips to jog her memory, then laughingly question whether the larger word and the smaller word on the sentence strip weren't the same. In each instance, she smiled ruefully, and read the sentence without hesitation.

Obviously, I had blundered by reducing the size of letters so drastically (from 2 inches down to 1 inch). However, the worst was probably over now, so, larger sentence strips wouldn't be cut.

Before bedtime, the children were shown the latter **h,** (sounded not as *aitch,* but as a quick exhalation of air) plus word slips for **hav** (*have*), **hat, it,** and **is.**

Our progress seems so slow and uncertain that I wonder if the best teaching method wouldn't be a mixture of the phonic method we are using, and the whole-word method we abandoned six months ago. I have just read a book recommending whole-word learning, and the results seem impressive. Perhaps I had made a mistake six months ago by teaching people's names instead of common words.

In the future, then, some time each session will be devoted to reading whole words without troubling to sound their individual letters, and this procedure will be carried on separately from our phonic exercises. In preparation, I printed the first sentence from the book *The Little Red Hen* in 2-inch letters on a 11½-by-17-inch sheet of paper: **Once upon a time there was a little red hen who lived in a farmyard.**

THE 23RD DAY

Our morning session featured new sentence strips (called here the B-sentences).

B-1.	wee see my fat cat	B-5.	see my bac
B-2.	I see my fat feet	B-6.	you hav my bus
B-3.	I hav biscits	B-7.	it is my hat
B-4.	my cat is sic		

Jean found the smaller type face easier to read and referred less often to the word slips. The children then recited the *Red Hen* sentence (for they knew it by heart) touching each word as they read it. Unfortunately, their fingers rarely touched the word being spoken.

We had just one session tonight, but it was a long one. The children's reading of the *Red Hen* sentence and the B sentences improved, though Jean had to resurrect word slips occasionally for the latter.

In bed, the children were shown the letter **o** (sounded as in *odd*, not *ode*), along with the words **soc** (*sock*), **hot,** and **cob.**[2] Eve quickly ascertained each word by sounding its letters.

THE 24TH DAY

The B sentence strips were reviewed this morning. Jean was in top form, but Eve lay on the floor beside the strips, yawning, and only the prospect of a cheese puff made her sit up and try to read. At that moment it occurred to me what a formidable task the reading program would have been without the use of rewards.

I read the *Red Hen* sentence along with the children, pointing to each word, **Once upon a time there was a little red hen who lived in a farmyard.** We repeated this step, then, finally, the children read the sentence by themselves while I pointed.

Next, we practiced sounding **o.** Eve and Jean were told to set their mouths in the shape of an **o** in order to sound the letter correctly, whereupon they hit on the idea of holding the printed **o** to their lips while sounding it.

The girls particularly liked **cob, hot,** and **soc,** perhaps because these words are more blustery than others (spoken quickly they sound like a locomotive starting up). A word slip for **this** was shown. Jean immediately asked me to form a

2. This word was known to the girls because cobs of corn were a favorite on their menu.

word train for **this is my hat,** then she read it. For some un-
known reason, Eve read the word **this** as **my,** then continued
to do so despite correction. Taking the **this** slip with us to the
car, I produced the word and sounded it about fifteen times
while driving, but when quizzed, Eve read it again as **my.** I
gasped an involuntary "Oh!" Strangely enough, this expression of disappointment had a good effect, for she began repeating **this** over and over to herself, and when quizzed again
later, identified the word correctly.

Realizing that I'd been missing a valuable opportunity to
continue the exercises during our four-minute drive to the
nursery, I clamped slips for **hot** and **this** to the sun visor this
afternoon and on the way home occasionally asked the girls
to identify them—a practice that yielded welcome relief from
the children's loud, frequently repetitious chatter. (Not that
multiple-use of the car was entirely new to me—two years
ten months earlier the same vehicle had served as a mater-
nity ward when Jean had occasioned my first and only lesson
in midwifery.)

Because the girls were very hungry, supper and baths took
priority over reading. After supper, Jean cried with tiredness
and discomfort from her sore throat. Eve, on the other hand,
wanted to play our games, and did so while Jean half-
reclined on the couch. Jean's illness must have aroused Eve's
maternal instinct, for she began sharing her rewards. (I increased the rewards proportionally to aid her support of a
dependent.)

The role of "provider" spurred Eve to greater effort, and
she occasionally stopped to let Jean know that more rewards
were coming. Jean reveled in her role of a tragically ill ward
and accepted each morsel calmly, as no more than was due
an invalid. Turning this motivationally rich situation to the
best advantage, I introduced three new sentences in the
hope they would end Eve's difficulty with **this:**

C-1.   this is a sic cat
C-2.   this is my soc
C-3.   this is a hot cob

Eve read the sentences flawlessly seven times each, and
one more problem seemed to be solved.

THE 25TH DAY

Morning sessions have run longer lately—about twenty to twenty-five minutes—to capitalize more fully on the children's freshness. They read the B and C sentence strips several times, the difficult ones more often than the others. Eve therefore read a total of forty-one sentences, and Jean (reading the C sentences for the first time), a total of fifty-four in all.

For me, the exercises are boring, and I sometimes forget to explode with jubilation when the children read a sentence correctly for the twentieth time—though the results are startling when I do. Indeed, Eve and Jean's enthusiasm ascends to its upper limit when father shifts from a merely pleased response to one that is dumbfounded.

When I called for the girls at the nursery this afternoon, the sun visor looked like a bulletin board. The words **cloc** (*clock*), **hil** (*hill*), and **lot** were clamped to it, as were the letters l and **I**. (To learn the letter l the children had to see how it differed from the capital **i**. Later, I would regret my decision to teach the lower-case letters first instead of the upper-case letters.) Neither Eve nor Jean could isolate and voice the l sound (sounded not as *ell*, but as at the end of *pill*), so they relied on the sound of the other letters in **cloc, hil,** and **lot** for identifying clues.

Enthusiasm waned during the trip home. Fortunately, another motivating trap had been baited in the form of two sheets of typing paper, one with Eve's name at the top, the other with Jean's, divided as illustrated (*Fig. 8*). Today's date had already been entered and a blue star had been attached to the first box to show that the morning session had been done. For the afternoon session, a star would be placed in the second box and an animal sticker placed in a larger box. Finally, before teeth brushing, a third star would be added plus a happy-face sticker (drawn with a marking pen on a red notarial seal).

Jean quickly read the B and C sentences several times and repeated any sentence she found difficult, reading altogether a total of forty-seven sentences. Eve, in a balky mood, finally came round when she saw the generous way cheesies were

Fig. 8

being handed out. Her incentive to read *all* the sentences
peaked when an animal picture was stuck on Jean's chart.

Eve continued to confuse **this** and **my**. Significantly, both
words had been learned as whole words instead of by sounding their letters, so I am beginning to question the value of
the *Red Hen* exercise. And I question it more when the chil-

dren sometimes become unlocked from the word sequence, and recite the rest of the sentence while pointing to wrong words.

Because the *Red Hen* sheet is so long (17 inches), the girls have had to kneel on the bottom line of lettering to reach the words on the top line. This problem has now been solved by attaching the sheet to the wall of our small foyer.

The session ended with readings of **hil, cloc,** and **lots.** The s was added to **lot** so as to conform with its most popular expression: "I want lots (of this or that preferred food)."

At eight o'clock, the children repeated the same exercises, then, with my help, decoded the following fourteen words printed in 1-inch letters on a piece of red construction paper.

milc (*milk*)	**leef** (*leaf*)	**loc** (*lock*)
wil (*will*)	**tee** (*tea*)	**litl** (*little*)
lic (*lick*)	**feel**	**seel** (the animal, *seal*)
meel (*meal*)	**il** (*ill*)	**cloc** (*clock*)
hil (*hill*)	**lots**	

THE 26TH DAY

The children's speed and ease of reading improved remarkably during our three sessions today, but Jean refused to sound letters in any word she couldn't immediately identify, and refused on the preposterous excuse that the word was one she has never seen before! A new sentence was introduced, **my litl cat feels il,** and for some reason, Eve couldn't remember **my.**

Eve was able to decode about half of the fourteen-word list; Jean wouldn't try. To acquaint the children with other letters, some of which may not be included in the exercises for weeks yet, the girls were periodically asked to try to isolate the beginning sounds of various words.

The charts proved their worth again tonight. Though full of energy for nonsense, the children lacked enthusiasm for reading until they were reminded it would yield a happy-face sticker.

THE 27TH, 28TH, AND 29TH DAYS

This Friday, Saturday, and Sunday were spent visiting friends. Even though our timetable was upset, we accomplished a lot. The children were shown the letter **p** (sounded not as *pea*, but as it sounds at the end of *stop*), plus word slips for **lap, lip, peel, hop,** and a new list of fourteen words in 1-inch type on the reverse side of the red construction paper:

pot	steep	pil (*pill*)
sip	stop	pupy (*puppy*)
slip	sleep	blac (*black*)
cap	clap	apl (*apple*)
hapy (*happy*)	hop	

The A and B sentences, now well learned, were set aside. Five new sentences were printed on colored strips and were added to the three **this** sentences, increasing our new working group to eight. Eve, the better decoder, read the new sentences without help.

C-1.	this is a sic cat	C-5.	wee wil see lots of hils
C-2.	this is my soc	C-6.	pic up this cloc
C-3.	this is a hot cob	C-7.	I hav a hot cup of tee
C-4.	my litl cat feels il	C-8.	my lip feels hot

The second sentence from the *Red Hen* story was printed on another 11½-by-17-inch sheet of paper—**One day the little red hen found some grains of wheat**—which the children had not learned to recite. They pointed to each word as I read it. Jean was able to read the sentence by herself in just two minutes; Eve took much longer.

Our rate of progress was now governed by the rate at which the children could learn new words, but Jean's reluctance to decode made the learning of new words slow and difficult. Until she could voice individual letters quickly, her ear would not be able to catch the sound of the complete word. How could Jean be taught to decode accurately and quickly?

During the three-hour drive home this afternoon, the girls, full from a hearty lunch, soon fell asleep on a mattress in the load area of the station wagon, leaving me to my thoughts up front. What would teach Jean to decode? Some pleasant repetitious, procedure was needed. For me, driving seems to favor problem solving. Not surprisingly, therefore, by the time we reached home, I had hit on a way to turn Jean into an enthusiastic decoder.

CHAPTER 8

The Mystifying Rectangle on the Refrigerator Door and Other Tales of Woe

Despite fourteen months difference in their ages, Eve and Jean are frequently mistaken for twins, and their mental performance is often as evenly matched as their physical appearance. In fact, as you have seen, Jean sometimes even surpasses her older sister. Competition between the two couldn't be keener if they were in fact twins, and the unending one-upmanship between them can be a tiring bother.

For example, the children had liked to run ahead of me down the long corridor from the elevator to our apartment, and vie for the privilege of turning the handle when the door was unlocked. In theory, the girls were to take turns operating the handle, but they could never remember whose turn it was, and I had enough on my mind without logging door openings. So I made a practice of hiding a coin in one hand, and the child who guessed which hand held the coin would open the door.

Unfortunately, if Eve lost, she became moody; if Jean lost, she cried. Even when, on subsequent occasions, the girls were reminded that one of them would have to lose graciously and a nod to this effect was exacted from each, the loser invariably responded with pouting or tears. The eventual solution was to prohibit either one from opening the door at all.

The inability to accept loss, though common among infants, may have been worsened in Eve and Jean's case by having a single parent. In any event, this touchy situation had to be allowed for when designing games for them. The children couldn't be pitted against each other in a way that permitted one to emerge a clear winner at the other's expense.

Also, any game procedure had to be extremely simple and, preferably, require some physical involvement. The game I was counting on to quickly increase Jean's decoding skill was an improved version of the marble game we had abandoned in the first few days of the program.

Four strips of orange-colored construction paper, 2½ inches by 10 inches, were folded in the middle to make tents standing almost 5 inches high. On the two outer surfaces of each tent, eight words were printed, four on each side, making a total of thirty-two words on all four tents (*Fig. 9*). The thirty-two words were drawn from the two fourteen-word lists (see pages 105 and 106) with two words—**leef** and **litl**—repeated, and the words **sily** (*silly*) and **hot** added. The tents were positioned in a spaced row, one side of each tent facing the children, who then took turns rolling a small car at them. If the car touched a tent, the child was permitted to sound, for a reward, the words on the side of the tent facing her.

Fig. 9. A tent.

Jean immediately wanted help with decoding, but then, for this help, she was obliged to repeat the decoding procedure unaided. Reasons could always be found to make her repeat words; for example, hesitation or overlooking a word, for which she then had to repeat all the words on that face of the tent.

When the car missed the tents occasionally, the value of winning a chance to sound the letters was increased. Within fifty minutes, Jean was decoding accurately and without hesitation. Reading of the *Red Hen* sentences seemed to progress equally well, and so the next line of the story was pinned to the wall: **She took them to the other animals in the farmyard.**

THE 30TH DAY

An old problem arose during our morning session: the children frequently missed the tents with the car, so I let them roll a chestnut—one of many we had gathered over the weekend. Unfortunately, the girls missed just as often with that. Eve and Jean were shown the single **e** (sounded not as *ee*, but as in *bet*) and word slips for **mes** (*mess*), **step,** and **best.**

For our presupper session, the children were given a golf ball to roll, and they hit the tents more often.

During supper I rashly announced that if the girls ate their entire meal they could play the game again. A regrettable promise! The children *didn't* eat their food yet wanted to play the game. The situation was distressing because we have a code, an established, unswerving policy, that father's promise of reward or punishment is always carried out exactly as described.

Finally, I backed off and grudgingly announced the session would have to be a very short one. With the code saved (if slightly bent), I could now work unobtrusively to lengthen the session. The ball-and-tent game so excited the children that they climbed onto my shoulders while waiting their turn.

Then, I thought of a dodge that would boost the efficiency of the game considerably. On their last turn, after about fifteen minutes of play, each child was permitted to read the words on *both* sides of any tent she hit for an additional reward; following which, they were allowed to read the words on *all* the tents at a payment of one reward for every four words. Eve and Jean ended with great mouthfuls of cheese puffs, having decoded as much during their final turn as they had during the entire game.

We turned to the three news words, **mes, step,** and **best,** and by simulating mock wonder and slight annoyance, I prompted the girls to sound each word twelve times. There is no knowing how long they might have continued the exercise. Being tired, I called a halt and stuck a blue star and a happy face to their charts.

THE 31ST DAY

The ball-and-tent game kept interest high for three profitable sessions today, and the children read the words so easily, one orange tent was removed, and two green tents with words containing **e** were added. Words used in the afternoon and evening sessions were:

pupy (*puppy*)	**blac** (*black*)	slip	steep	sleep
cap	**loc** (*lock*)	**seel** (*seal*)	hil	**litl** (*little*) [1]
leef (*leaf*)	**il** (*ill*)	**milc** (*milk*)	**sily** (*silly*)	hot
hop	**litl** (*little*) [1]	pot	**apl** (*apple*)	sip
pil (*pill*)	stop	clap	**hapy** (*happy*)	pet
sel (*sell*)	**tel** (*tell*)	**wel** (*well*)	toilet	**bel** (*bell*)
bucet (*bucket*)	wet	best	**mes** (*mess*)	step
bascet (*basket*)	**fel** (*fell*)	**pocet** (*pocket*)	met	let

1. The word **litl** was one of the two words duplicated on the first four orange tents.

On their last turn each game the children were allowed to read all other words on the tents—a total of forty—for ten rewards. Jean now sounds letters and reads words as easily as Eve. The **oi** diphthong in **toilet** proved difficult for both girls, and Eve occasionally confused **f** and **t**, probably because of the crossbar.

The letter **n** was introduced (sounded as it does at the end of *sun*) along with slips bearing the words **fun, nap,** and **nec** *(neck)*. Another sentence from *The Red Hen* was posted: **"Who will help me to plant these grains of wheat?" asked the little red hen.** The girls were told to ignore the quotation marks and the question mark. Apparently, the *Red Hen* sentences have increased Jean's reading vocabulary, for she pointed out, on request, the words **who** and **found.**

THE 32ND DAY

The three remaining orange tents were removed from our half-hour game this morning, and the two green tents (words containing **e**) were supplemented by a red tent and a yellow tent bearing words containing **n**:

on	pen	in	upon	man
pin	ten	anty *(auntie)*	nap	win
sun	can	fun	not	nec *(neck)*
nee *(knee)*				

The children occasionally confused **p** and **b**, which makes me want to delay the introduction of **d** all the longer. Jean read the *Red Hen* sentences much better than Eve, who frequently spoke words while pointing to others (then resented correction).

There were no requests for the game this afternoon, and, wanting a rest, I said nothing. After supper, when the girls asked to play, they were told that a good performance of the ball-and-tent game would win them an introduction to a new letter. That tore it! Jean confused **f** for **t** (and vice versa) and began reading **let** as **wet**. Eve sounded **n** as **h** (or, for diversion, as an **l**), then began reading **man** as **mes.**

Eve's errors eventually became so absurd I tried to halt the proceedings. Alas, this merely spurred her to greater effort and greater error, reading **can** as **cap**. Finally, the children's attention was diverted to the *Red Hen* sentences and they read these so well, the fifth installment of the story was posted: "**Not I**," **said the cat, "Not I**," **said the rat, "Not I**," **said the pig.**

Hoping the girls had forgotten that the introduction of a new letter had been contingent upon a good performance of the ball-and-tent game, I showed them the letter **g** (sounded not as *jee*, but as the final sound in *egg*), along with word slips bearing **big, gas,** and **gum.** The children sounded each new word fourteen times, until I, yawning, ended the lesson.

THE 33RD DAY

We reviewed the five parts of the *Red Hen* story twice during a twenty-five-minute morning session, then went on to the sixth part: "**Then I shall plant the grains of wheat myself**," **said the little red hen. So she did.** During the day, I reduced the first three sentences of the *Red Hen* story by half—to letters ⅞ inch high—and they fitted snugly on a single piece of typing paper.

The afternoon session started badly and quickly deteriorated. For openers, the children wouldn't pay attention while the words on the two new **g** tents were being introduced:

fog	**hog**	**tenis** (*tennis*)	**rug**	**gum**
got	**gon** (*gone*)	**gul** (*gull*)	**peg**	**pig**
gas	**get**	**leg**	**bug**	**bag**
big				

The word **rug** was included to introduce **r.** The word **gull** could be included because seagulls, searching for worms and grubs turned up by the plows, were frequent visitors to the farm.

In their own way, the children managed to plow up the ball-and-tent game by confusing **p** and **b** and by mispronouncing **u** and **e.** In addition, Eve pronounced **l** as **n,** and even spelled and read **nap** as **man.** Strangely enough, when I finally exploded (which I report with embarrassment), she was able to read the word correctly. Next, Jean complained of thirst, and given a drink, then knocked over the sheet of masonite used to prevent the golf ball from rolling under the couch. The atmosphere was becoming charged, and only by great effort was I able to end the session amicably.

THE 34TH DAY

No request for the game was formally lodged this morning. Indeed, when I broached the matter of cheesies in my most engaging manner, it drew silence from Eve and a flat "No" from Jean. But when asked if they would like to read the *Red Hen* sentences on the wall, the response was enthusiastic, and they were soon cramming cheese puffs by the fistful into their mouths.

Now, with their stomachs as eager allies, I turned to the tent game and, after a few minutes of play, let the children read all sides of the tents for one reward per side. The girls read with precision, and by doing so, atoned for the psychological drubbing I had suffered at their hands last night. I felt comfortably in command of the situation again, equal to, and ready for, their next terrible surprise.

A game was needed to give the children better recognition of the *Red Hen* words, which they were, in the main, merely mouthing. The girls knew the text by heart, but their ability to identify individual *Red Hen* words was poor.

The game that gradually took shape in my mind seemed to have every feature imaginable—high visual appeal, simplicity, brisk rate of progress, plus the fascinating manipulation of magnets for markers. Such was the apparent promise of the "refrigerator game."

With a sense of triumph, I glued twenty irregularly shaped pieces of variously colored paper on the refrigerator door in the shape of a rectangle 16 inches by 12 inches. The sequence of colors changed around the rectangle, as in a rainbow, to provide a visually pleasing effect. In random order, words from the *Red Hen* story were printed with a grease

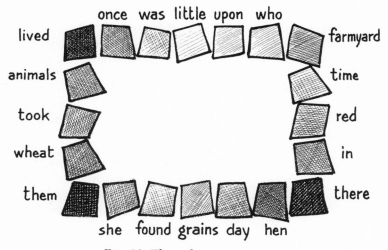

Fig. 10. The refrigerator game.

marking-crayon on the refrigerator door, one word beside each piece of colored paper (*Fig. 10*). The top-left corner of the rectangle—**lived**—was to be the starting point. The children would take turns rolling a die [2] and move their own small marker magnet around the rectangle according to their roll, counting every colored piece of paper as a "position." When their marker came to rest, the children would then read the word beside each colored position they had passed.

The refrigerator game was an immediate winner when the children spied it. On being told they could play this new game as a bonus following "tents" and reading the "book," Eve and Jean fairly flew into their exercises.

Just how badly we needed a game for the *Red Hen* words was emphasized by Eve who pointed to each word in the sentence **One day the little red hen found some grains of wheat,** while reciting "**Who will help me to plant these grains of wheat?**" With haste and with hope I turned the girls to the new game on the refrigerator.

I wish I could report that the refrigerator game set us rac-

_____
2. Half a pair of dice.

ing down the road to literacy. Matters went otherwise. First of all, the business of teaching the children to roll and count the die proved to be a bigger job than I'd imagined. After five minutes of instruction, I sensed futility and simply promised to help the girls calculate their moves.

To begin, Jean rolled a six—a disaster, for, in order to move six positions, she would have to read the first six words— **lived, who, once, was, little, farmyard.** While coaching Jean, I also coached Eve, who in her turn would have to go over the same route. After five minutes of questioning and prompting Jean, she knew the six words, but Eve could manage only the first two. More coaching and Eve had learned the third word. After a few more minutes the fourth word was fixed in her mind. But now she'd forgotten the first word. I felt as if I had one foot in a canoe that was easing away from the dock. Wearing a fixed grin, I turned the children's attention to supper.

THE 35TH DAY—SATURDAY

The morning session began with a review of thirteen old sentence strips picked at random from among the A and B sentences.

I am sic	I see biscits	wee see my fat cat
I see my fat feet	you see a scab	wee see a tub
see my scab	you hav my bus	wee see a cub
I see a mat	see my bac	you see a bus
I see you		

Surprisingly, the children read these with a great deal of hesitation. Worse, Eve had forgotten **you** and **my.** But these were mere peccadilloes compared to the outrages she committed during the tent game. Though the words were all familiar ones, Eve pronounced **ns** as **hs**, sounded the letters, then read **leg** as **nec, pen** as **big** or **beg**, occasionally sounded **n** as **g**, and was joined by Jean in confusing **p** and **b**.

The children then read the "book." My faith in the *Red Hen* sentences has, however, diminished, because the reading of them seems to be no more than an exercise in eye movement across descending lines of text.

Jean and I played three circuits of the refrigerator game. She recognized half the words, but still couldn't count the dots on the die.

Efficiency of the tent game was doubled during a later session by requiring both sides of a tent to be read when hit by the ball. I wondered if some of the puzzling errors that occurred during the game arose from the words having become somehow stale for the children. Whatever the reason, Eve and Jean's performance was getting worse, so other tents containing new words were prepared.

THE 36TH DAY—SUNDAY

Most of the day was spent visiting friends, but in our 5:30 session, the letter **r** was formally introduced (the children had already encountered **r** in **rug**), and sounded as it is at the end of *her*. The girls played ball and tents with three new **r** tents and two new **g** tents presenting the following words:

run	free	tric (*trick*)	bring	ring
rist (*wrist*)	rong (*wrong*)	rub	string	crib
fast	bric (*brick*)	strong	street	brecfast (*breakfast*)
trip	truc (*truck*)	rat	roc (*rock*)	ran
eg (*egg*)	top	frog	green	

THE 37TH DAY

Jean, barely awake, wanted to play "the game" (meaning tents). Instead, she and Eve were induced to review the thirteen A and B sentence strips they had read so hesitatingly on Saturday (see page 116). While Eve was reading **you see a bus** I glanced down, and to my astonishment, saw that the strip was positioned upside down. Until then, I'd been only half awake. When I righted the strip and asked Eve to read it again, she read **a** as **my**.

Eve still can't recognize individual words in the *Red Hen* sentences, and because it seemed unlikely she would ever master the refrigerator game, we clearly needed another game to help her recognize words. An adaptation of the game Concentration seemed to offer a combination of simplicity, repetition, and fun, so the word **once** was printed on two cards, **time** on two others, and **upon** on two more.

The game went as follows. The cards were turned word side down on the floor, and one child was allowed to turn over any two cards and read them. If the words were the same, she picked up the cards; if different, she turned the two cards down again and let her sister turn up any two cards of her choice. More cards would be added to the game when the children developed skill and gained confidence with the first six.

Simple though the game seemed, the children made every mistake imaginable. They read words backward, upside down, and confused many of the letters. Words the children had identified easily in the tent game—**truc, roc, ring**—were substituted, with no benefit. In desperation, I substituted the long-familiar words **cab, you,** and **see.** The game finally proceeded, but did so at a very slow rate. The children could neither understand the rules, nor manipulate the cards properly. I began to suspect that by the time Eve and Jean mastered the workings of this particular game, they would have gained sufficient skill from the phonic side of our program to read the *Red Hen* words without need of a word-recognition game.

The word **where** was added to the sun visor, and the girls identified it several times during our drive to the nursery.

This afternoon, after the children had been washed, rinsed, drained, and dried, they reviewed **where,** then read three new sentence strips: **where is the fat frog** (D-1); **where is my big pig** (D-2); **where is my litl cat** (D-3). The other thirteen mixed A and B sentence strips (see page 116) were set out, and the children read the total sixteen sentences three times each. I was astounded by the ease with which Eve could read sentences positioned upside down. Thinking she just couldn't be bothered turning the strips around, I established the rule that sentences had to be read in the normally accepted manner to qualify for a reward. But now the preposterous truth became apparent: she couldn't tell for sure whether a sentence was upside down or not, and I, as a self-styled upside-down adviser, had to tell her at least a dozen times to turn a sentence strip around.

The tent game followed, but this soon had to be stopped despite Eve's objection because the lesson had run an hour and fifteen minutes.

Tonight, as a respite from mealtime babbling, arguing, and giggling, I introduced the word **like** while the children ate, and printed the sentence **I like big trees** (D-4) on a strip 2 inches by 10 inches. The children decoded this without help, then asked me to print **I like big biscits** (D-5) and **I like blac dogs** (D-6) on other strips (**dogs** forced me to introduce the letter **d**).

Just before bedtime, the children read the sentences D-1 to D-6, and the thirteen mixed A and B sentence strips to earn their third blue star and happy face. Eve persisted in occasionally reading strips positioned upside down, and I grew weary of telling her to turn the strips around.

When the girls were asleep, I printed the first three *Red Hen* sentences in ¼-inch type, all on half a sheet of typing paper. The next three segments of the story, presently pinned on the walls of the foyer, were reduced from 1-inch letters down to ½-inch, and they barely fitted on an 8½-by-11-inch sheet. Finally, the contents of the thirteen mixed A and B sentence strips were printed in letters ⁹/₁₆ inch high as a list on a sheet of typing paper, this being a one-half reduction in type size from the letters on the sentence strips. A major benefit in grouping the sentences on a single sheet would be that once the list was correctly positioned, Eve would read all the sentences right side up.

THE 38TH DAY

Jean wandered sleepily out from her bedroom and began reading the *Red Hen* sentences, now extending along one wall of the tiny box-shaped foyer, across the hall door and along the other wall.

After breakfast, the children read the thirteen A and B sentence strips, then read the same sentences again but in the reduced type size on the newly printed list. Unfortunately, only a single space had been left between the sentences, and the children had difficulty tracking each line of print across the page without wandering onto the line above or below.

The sentence list, eliminating as it did the need to pick up and position individual sentence strips, reduced the time for this exercise by a whopping two thirds.

Sentences D-1 to D-6 were read, then the reduced version of the first three *Red Hen* sentences. Luckily *two* spaces had been left between each line of lettering here, so Jean read the text easily without straying off the lines. Eve read only the large original 11½-inch-by-17-inch version, but even so she still had difficulty with the sixth group: "**Then I shall plant the grains myself,**" **said the little red hen. So she did.**

The list of thirteen mixed A and B sentences (hereafter called thirteen AB list) were printed again, this time in letters $^7/_{16}$ inch high with *two* spaces between the lines, and during our forty-five-minute session before supper, the children read the list easily. The girls then read thirteen of the other old sentence strips (the eight C sentences, page 107, plus five A and B sentences that hadn't been included in the earlier group of thirteen sentences), and the six D sentence strips for a total reading of thirty-two different sentences (13 + 13 + 6).

Much was accomplished during a brief aftersupper session. The children read the same thirty-two sentences again plus the *Red Hen* sentences. Eve provided a stunning assortment of surprises. The list of thirteen AB sentences was upside down to her when she accepted it from Jean. Sensing the need for repositioning, Eve turned the sheet of paper a quarter turn and began reading the sentences *vertically*. She had read two sentences in this way, without error, before I realized what was happening. When asked to turn the page another quarter turn and start again, Eve began introducing a profusion of errors: she read **sic** as **mad**, and **a** as **my**. However, the biggest surprise came while reading '**where is my big pig.** Though the strip was positioned correctly for her, Eve began reading it mirror fashion—**gip gib ym** . . .

At bedtime the children were usually allowed to "read" books for a few minutes before the light was turned out—a period, in truth, devoted more to looking at picture books and occasionally recognizing words. Jean surprised me tonight by reading the first two sentences from the published book *The Little Red Hen*.

While they nodded off, I printed, on a sheet of typing paper in ¼-inch letters, a second list of thirteen more sentences taken from the colorful strips (eight C sentences plus the five A and B sentences that hadn't been included in the first list) and these were then glued back to back with that earlier list of thirteen AB sentences. So now, twenty-six of the children's first sentences were contained in a reduced form on two sides of a single composite sheet.

THE 39TH DAY

We had overslept, so there was just time for a quick breakfast before setting off into the fog—the fourth such morning in a row. Despite the day's forbidding start the weather changed and, in doing so, indirectly influenced our reading accomplishments for the day. Sunny weather prevailed, and the temperature actually climbed back into the seventies! This warm October treat, a respite from a long (and usually

bitterly cold) winter, called for an active demonstration of gratitude. We took a different route homeward through the farm, left the car at the arboretum, and soon the three of us were chasing a large beach ball down the leave-strewn hills onto a grassy expanse bordering Dow's Lake.

I confess to extending our football game as long as possible to tire the girls for bed, but the forty minutes of fun was to yield quite a different bonus.

On arriving home the children's first need was a bath. Then, because of all the running, they clamored for food. But supper was still cooking, so Eve and Jean were induced to read the twenty-six sentences (the two back-to-back lists). And they read with such ease and eagerness they were allowed to read the sentences again—whereupon the girls surprised me more by preferring to play tents for fifteen minutes even though supper was now ready.

Perhaps this was a mute comment on my cooking. In any event, Eve and Jean had never read more quickly or more correctly before. Their excellent performance seemed a fitting end to a memorable Indian summer day.

THE 40TH DAY

This morning, fortified by a nameless porridge-raisin-date-honey conglomerate, the children read the twenty-six sentences twice each, then two new ones—**my ring is in this green bag** (D-7) and **this is the rong street** (D-8)—after which they were formally introduced to the letter **d**, though they had already encountered **d** in **did, dog,** and **red.** As expected, the children confused **d** with **b,** so a dot was placed above the bulb of the **d** to distinguish it, and the girls were alerted to the fact that the word **dot** itself began with the **d** sound.

Our sole session this evening was given over to general review. Eve still couldn't read the first three *Red Hen* sentences in ½-inch letters, whereas Jean read them in 14-point type ($^5/_{32}$ inch) from the published book itself.

THE 41ST DAY

There was little interest in reading this morning until I read thirteen sentences quickly and paid myself a cheese puff. Surprised and delighted, the girls joined me and read well.

Eve knows the letter sounds so well now that she rarely voices them before reading the whole word. Then why can't she read the *Red Hen* sentences? Jean occasionally sounds the letters in even simple words (however, I suspect she does this more from habit than from need). In any case, every time Jean stopped to sound individual letters, she was asked to read the entire sentence again without stopping.

Sometimes, when Eve reads sentences incorrectly—for example, **I see scabs** for **I see beets**—and I say "No," she unhesitatingly reads the sentence correctly. One sentence that is never fumbled is **pic up that cloc,** which was, oddly enough, one of the last of the twenty-six (back to back) sentences learned.

The children didn't want to play tents but, stimulated by nonsense, they began. After a few minutes, they were permitted to stockpile rewards by reading all the tents. The girls were reluctant to read the eight D sentences. Again, they were activated by tomfoolery.

We seemed to have reached an all-time low this session, with Eve and Jean unenthusiastic at its beginning, middle, and end. Before wrapping up the lesson and figuratively dropping it in the garbage, I showed the children the word **want.** They blinked alertly and asked me to print two new sentences—**I want a truc** (D-9) and **I want a doly** (D-10)—so we ended with a small gain.

The tent game had now served its purpose. More would be gained by employing as many tent words as possible in sentences. Four new D sentences were composed and printed on strips, raising the total number of strips in use to fourteen:

D-1.	where is the fat frog	D-4.	I like big trees
D-2.	where is my big pig	D-5.	I like big biscits
D-3.	where is my litl cat	D-6.	I like blac dogs

D-7. my ring is in this green bag
D-8. this is the rong street
D-9. I want a truc
D-10. I want a doly

D-11. giv him his boots
D-12. bring your pants here
D-13. I can run very fast
D-14. this string is very strong

Special attention was given to the two words the children hadn't seen before—**boots** and **here**.

The children's reading of the twenty-six sentences improved still more tonight, but much enticement was necessary before they would attempt sentences D-1 to D-14. Because serifs [3] had been omitted from the **I**s when the sentences had been printed smaller, the girls confused **I**s and **l**s. Serifs were now added (*Fig. 11*).

Fig. 11

A major weakness in our program is that the children must read sentences they have largely memorized. In an ideal exercise, the girls would read a variety of sentences composed of the same words in different combinations, but this would entail a formidable job of hand lettering.

Fortunately, I had six hours of driving this long week end, and during the trip managed to think up not only a way to produce a great variety of different sentences quickly, but also plans for another game that would ultimately teach the children new words at the astonishing rate of one a minute.

3. Serifs are the small projections that can be seen at the top and bottom of many letters.

CHAPTER 9

Whatever Became of the Abominable Liozebrilla?

THE 42ND DAY—SATURDAY

A popular children's plaything years ago was a booklet in which all pages had been cut horizontally into three separate sections. The heads of various animals were depicted on all the top sections, their bodies were shown on the middle sections, legs and feet were on the lower sections. By turning the sections independently of each other, different body parts could be mixed and matched to form a great number of curious creatures—for example, one having the head of a lion, the body of a zebra, and the arms and legs of a gorilla (*Fig. 12*).

What delight these ridiculous creatures evoked! However, my interest now lay in the great number of variations that could be composed with only a few interchanging parts. For example, by cutting three animals into thirds, twenty-seven other animals could be formed. If this same idea could be used to form sentences, then many different sentences could be composed easily and quickly from just a few components.

My mind fastened onto this idea as we began a 150-mile journey, and I puzzled over a possible solution as the children slept in the back (a condition that had been secured by feeding them a large lunch before leaving, then turning the

Fig. 12. A liozebrilla.

car heater on full). Could a variety of sentences be composed from just a few beginnings, a few middles, and a few endings?

A piece of plywood wedged between the seat and the dashboard served as my traveling desk. Here I could jot down notes without taking my eyes off the road. Today, I puzzled out and scribbled down six possible sentence beginnings, middles, and endings:

would you like	fish	today
we would like	bread	for supper
we will have	jelly	now
will we have	beets	soon
can I have	eggs	for lunch
do you want	carrots	for breakfast

The children would have to learn eleven new words for the exercise, after which the interchangeable parts would permit the composition of 216 different sentences. I bought the materials at a general store on our route—a spiral-bound school exercise book and a felt-tip marking pen—and on arriving at the home of our hosts, cut six pages of the exercise book into three sections each and printed the six sentence beginnings, middles, and endings on them (*Fig. 13*). Only correct spelling was used, and the children accepted easily the extra letters now in **have, will, egg, breakfast.** The new

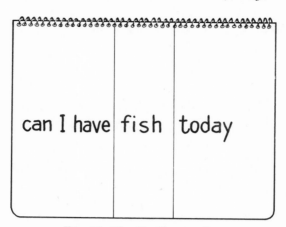

Fig. 13. The flip-flop reader.

device—called the "flip-flop" reader—was presented to the girls as if it were a trick of magic, and they responded by sucking their breath excitedly as each new sentence was formed.

Whenever the children found a section of any sentence difficult, that part was left exposed, and another part of the sentence was flipped to other familiar material. Repetition of the difficult material was thus secured in a nonboring way. Only one of the three sections was ever changed at a time, so, with every change, the children had already successfully read two thirds of the new sentence formed. Difficult words and phrases were not changed until they became easy. Altogether, half the components were introduced this session (though not every possible combination of them), and Eve and Jean learned five new words while reading fifty different sentences.

THE 43RD DAY—SUNDAY

The children learned the remaining six new words in the flip-flop reader and were allowed to play "teacher"—that is, to take turns flipping over the page sections and paying a reward for each correct reading of the sentences formed. This novelty yielded two benefits: the children's enthusiasm was increased by their taking an active part in the instruction and the "teacher" herself had to read the material to know whether the reward had been earned. The sole disadvantage accrued to the exercise book, for it quickly deteriorated under the children's rough, sticky-fingered handling.

The flip-flop reading went so well, additional pages were sectioned and new sentence components were printed: **I want, may I have, apples, stew, corn,** and **pumpkin.** Though the new material created immediate interest, it required greater effort, so interest soon waned. The children's enthusiasm was secured for the evening session by starting with easier material—eight of the D sentence strips. Surprisingly, Jean substituted **rope** for **string** in the sentence **this string is very strong** though they haven't been taught to read **rope** yet. The girls then read the easier composite sentences; Eve wanted to play "teacher," but Jean refused to participate, so I, filling a curious role, had to call Eve "teacher" while telling her which components to change and read. Jean then read the *Red Hen* book, Eve read the enlarged version of it.

THE 44TH DAY

Our well-intentioned hostess stuffed Eve and Jean so full of pancakes and syrup that the girls rose from the breakfast table with glazed eyes and remained beyond the temptation of raisins for an hour and a half; hunger then prompted them to review the D sentences. Three new sentence strips were introduced, composed mostly of tent words.

> **D-15.** I went on a long trip
> **D-16.** did you see the red bird
> **D-17.** jean ran acros the gras

The girls read the flip-flop composite sentences, after which Jean progressed to the next page of the *Red Hen* book: **Everyday the little red hen went to the field to watch the grains of wheat growing. They grew tall and strong.** Eve read haltingly from the large *Red Hen* sheets.

Why was Eve having such difficulty with the *Red Hen* sentences? Why, in fact, were both children sometimes uncertain when identifying individual words in these sentences? Perhaps I had erred by teaching whole sentences at a time instead of just whole words. We had games for the phonic side of our reading program but none—except the unsuccessful refrigerator game—for the whole-word side. We needed an engaging game that would present the *Red Hen* material as single words. Our long return trip this afternoon provided an opportunity to think about such a game. The one that finally came to mind seemed to combine repetition, simplicity, and fun; I began constructing it as soon as we arrived home.

A strip of white cardboard, 8 inches by 32 inches, was

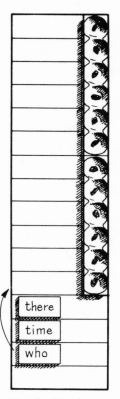

Fig. 14. The blocks game.

ruled every 2 inches of its length to form sixteen sections. An egg carton, its lid removed, was cut lengthwise between the rows of cups, and these were then glued to the cardboard to form a single row of twelve receptacles. The words **there, time,** and **who** were printed in letters ⅝ inch high on three cards and attached with mounting putty to three toy building blocks [1] which were then positioned as shown in the illustration for the start of the game (*Fig. 14*). A raisin was placed in each of the twelve eggcups.

To play the game (which we simply called "blocks"), one child was to read the three words, move the block nearest her in a jump over the other two, place it beside the first cup, read the words again, then take the raisin in that cup. The other child would similarly read the three words, move the block nearest her over the other two, place it opposite the second cup, read the words again, and help herself to the raisin. During the game each child had six turns, and, in reading the words twice each time, they read each word a total of twelve times.

Eve had great difficulty distinguishing between the three words, so I coached her before beginning a second game. But two false starts and an additional fifteen minutes of coaching, confirmed the fact that she simply wasn't able to distinguish between the words **there** and **time.** Finally **was** was substituted for **there,** and the girls had a pleasant game, followed by yet a third one.

Though the children were extremely tired after their supper and bath, they wanted to play blocks again. But it was too late.

THE 45TH DAY

The children composed sentences in the flip-flop reader then played blocks with the words **who, time,** and **was.** The first two cups held raisins, the next two peanuts, the next two cheese puffs, and this same sequence was repeated in the other six cups.

1. Blocks were used so the children would be able to manipulate the words more easily.

A fourth word, **lived,** was added for their second game. But now, strangely, Eve couldn't remember **time.** Considering she had already identified **time** thirty-six times in previous games of blocks and read it on numerous occasions in the *Red Hen* sentences, her sudden lapse of memory was discouraging. I interrupted the game twice to drill her in recognizing **time,** and she improved slightly.

The children obviously needed coaching for a couple of minutes before the start of every session. I begin to see the futility of assessing what the girls *should* remember. Infants apparently learn in a manner totally different from adults, and there's not much to be done about it but accept the fact. Hoping that more frequent exposure of the words would hasten easy identification, I fastened the words **lived, time, was,** and **who** to the sun visor before picking up the girls this afternoon.

Jean ate no supper and complained of being tired. Eve played blocks, and shared her rewards.

THE 46TH DAY

Although fever from the flu eroded my patience today, we had a good morning session reviewing the twenty-six back-to-back sentences, then the flip-flop sentences, and finally blocks, in which the word **upon** was substituted for **who.** Instead of immediately eating their rewards, the children saved them on a plate, then, to my surprise, ended by leaving a cheese puff, two nuts and a raisin.

Lacking sufficient initiative to produce artwork, I spent part of the day revising the reading materials. The twenty-six sentences were reduced in size from $^7/_{16}$-inch type to $^5/_{16}$-inch. The simplified spelling was now corrected and capital letters were placed at the beginning of each sentence. In all, forty-one typographical changes were made (*Fig. 15*).

By adding the components, **could I have, for dinner,** and **this morning** to the flip-flop reader, 720 different sentences could now be composed (nine beginnings, ten middles, eight endings). To provide the children with a quick review of

7/16"   **my litl cat f**

5/16"   My little cat feels

Fig. 15

these various parts, ten sentences were composed and printed on a sheet of paper:

E-1.   Would you like apples for dinner?
E-2.   We would like fish today.
E-3.   We will have bread for supper.
E-4.   Will we have jelly now?
E-5.   Can I have beets soon?
E-6.   Do you want eggs for lunch?
E-7.   May I have carrots for breakfast?
E-8.   I want stew this morning.
E-9.   I would like corn for supper.
E-10. Could I have banana for lunch?

The seventeen D sentences, still on colored strips, were now printed with corrected spelling and with capitals at the beginning of each sentence (twenty-three typographical changes in all) in 5/16-inch letters on a sheet of typing paper.

D-1.   I like black dogs.
D-2.   I like big biscuits.
D-3.   I like big trees.
D-4.   Where is the fat frog?
D-5.   Where is my little cat?
D-6.   Where is my big pig?
D-7.   My ring is in this green bag.
D-8.   This is the wrong street.
D-9.   I want a truck.
D-10. I want a dolly.
D-11. Give him his boots.
D-12. Bring your pants here.
D-13. I can run very fast.

D-14.   This string is very strong.
D-15.   I went on a long trip.
D-16.   Did you see the red bird?
D-17.   Jean ran across the grass.

Finally, the *Red Hen* sentences on the second sheet were reduced in size (*Fig. 16*).

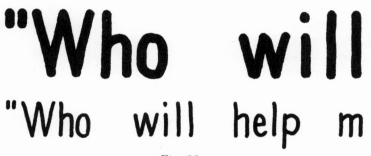

"**Who will**
"Who will help m

Fig. 16

The children were naturally puzzled by the appearance of capital letters—particularly **M, D, G, B, T**—but they readily accepted my explanation that these symbols were merely other ways to show **m, d, g, b, t**. The question marks were also explained. Their reading of the twenty-six back-to-back sentences, now in smaller letters, was good, but the girls read the seventeen D sentences with much hesitation and error. The corrected spelling received a mixed reaction: neither child was able to identify **wrong** until the **w** was covered; however, many corrections, such as those occurring in **tea, biscuits, grass,** and **across** went unnoticed.

The session after supper would best be forgotten. Despite the children's many readings of **was**—in the *Red Hen* sentences, in the refrigerator game, in several games of blocks, and on the sun visor—neither child could now recognize the word. Fortunately, they seemed to gain total recall of **was** when told it.

The girls were shown **there** on a block, and after a few exercises, we began a game. Unfortunately, they kept forgetting the word, so we had more drills and attempted another game.

But now, Jean began forgetting **was** again. My fever and headache suddenly seemed too oppressive to continue; I terminated the session with as much dignity as I could muster and looked forward to better days.

THE 47TH DAY

We had time for only one game of blocks this morning. The word **there** was shown occasionally and the girls seemed to have learned it by the end of the session.

The more outlandish the assortment of rewards in the eggcups, the greater the children's enthusiasm for playing blocks. This afternoon, in addition to raisins, peanuts, and cheese puffs, the eggcups contained postage-stamp-sized pieces of toast and morsels of cheese; fragments of cookies provided an introductory special in the first two cups.

This Lilliputian banquet, replenished for their second game, resulted in our having a particularly long, successful session reviewing all the material. Not that the session was without its quaint collection of problems: while reading the sentence lists, Jean's eyes strayed onto the sentences above or below the one she was reading. Eve was still puzzled by the capital letters **T, M, D, G,** and she repeatedly forgot **there** in two games of blocks. The children clamored to play a third game; but because it was late they were allowed only half a game.

THE 48TH DAY

Three blocks bearing two words each were used in the game this morning—**upon, time; there, was; who, lived.** Neither child had remembered **there** but recalled the word easily on hearing it. Later in the game, a fourth block bearing **found** was added and the children learned it so easily that **once** was introduced on a fifth block. But now the girls began to falter, so **once** was removed.

The children took turns being teacher while playing blocks, and supervised each other so well that I was able to leave them and tend to other chores. Pieces of date, included among the rewards for the first time, were a hit.

We reached another low tonight. Perhaps my patience is running out. The children still confused some of the capital letters—Eve more than Jean. But worse, Eve actually couldn't read the word a in **I want a truck.** She had, by now, correctly read the word at least *two hundred* times. Exasperated, I took the list from her but she made such a fuss I relented and let her continue. However, on reading the very next sentence, she stopped again at the same word and looked at me with a helpless smile. I sounded a so loudly she jumped. Feeling wretched, I snapped the list from her and began reading the newspaper.

After cooling off for five minutes, I let Jean read the ten E sentences. Unfortunately, her eyes continued to stray onto lines above and below the one she was reading. Eve began again and read much better.

Parts of a new series of composite sentences printed in another part of the flip-flop reader were now introduced.

a red bird	has been	swimming
your black cat	is	skipping
our big dog	likes	eating
that old hen	was	jumping
the baby pig	isn't	singing
this fat bear	wasn't	running
my little dolly	will be	hopping
the tall monster		dancing
the elephant		flying
my sister		sleeping
Daddy		crying
who		hiding
		sitting
		shopping

The new sentence parts proved too difficult for the children so we turned to blocks, and during two and a half games the words **found, once,** and **she** were included. The words **who, there, was, time** were contained on a single block, and

Fig. 17

by doubling up other words, just three blocks—four at the most—were ever needed for the nine *Red Hen* words now in the game (*Fig. 17*).

THE 49TH DAY—SATURDAY

In our tiny apartment, enforced proximity to the children on week ends strains my patience. Indeed, my patience almost ruptured during our first session today, held when the girls awoke from their noon nap.

The seventeen D and the ten E sentences had been lettered again in a smaller type, with three spaces between each line, and Jean had no difficulty tracking sentences across the page (*Fig. 18*). Eve introduced a stunning assortment of errors; she forgot **Did, My, Where, Give,** and **This,** and did so in a smiling, unconcerned manner. The tension eased when the girls began playing blocks. In fact, the game proceeded so well the block bearing **upon** and **lived** was replaced by one bearing **grains.**

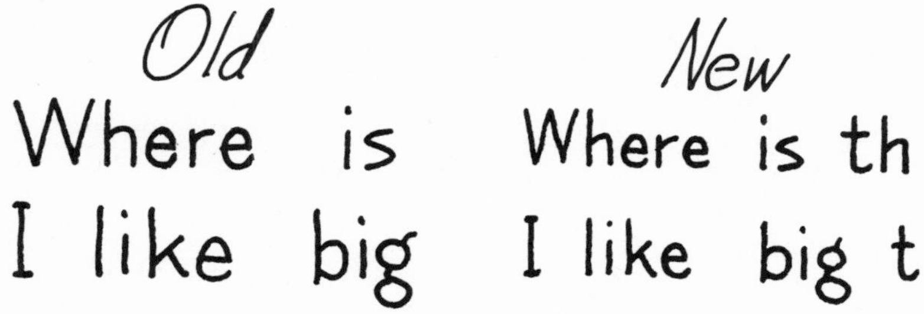

Old

New

Where is   Where is th

I like big   I like big t

Fig. 18

Because Jean didn't eat her supper, rewards with high nutritional value were employed in the game before bedtime: grapes, dates, and biscuits. Eve had difficulty with a new word, **will**, and still couldn't identify it at the end of the game—a failure made more puzzling by the fact that **wil** had been among the first words learned in the tent game; moreover, the children had read it easily on numerous occasions in the E sentences **We will have bread for supper** and **Will we have jelly now?** In fact, **will** had been included in the game of blocks only by error!

To determine how much the children had learned by reading the *Red Hen* sentences, thirty-six words from the story were printed in the form of a jumbled list, and the girls were tested separately on their recognition of the words. I was stung to discover that each child could identify but twelve words; and the only words they commonly identified were eight that had been used in the game of blocks. Seemingly, the time and effort spent printing the various enlargements of the *Red Hen* sentences, coaching the girls, listening to and correcting them, hadn't added a single word to their reading vocabulary.

The whole-word method of reading obviously works, as is clearly seen by the blocks game. But the children had learned only eight words in four and a half days; and this, despite their great knowledge of phonics. Apparently, knowledge of phonics—unexercised—does little to hasten the learning of words as wholes.

Acting on a hunch, I printed the word **dogs**. Eve couldn't identify it, though Jean could. I printed **bird** and neither child recognized it. My suspicion was well founded. Though the children had apparently read both words correctly many times in the D sentences **I like black dogs** and **Did you see the red bird?**—they had merely been reciting completions to **I like black** and **Did you see the red** with scarcely a glance at **dogs** or **bird.**

But the more curious fact was that **dogs** and **bird**, though both phonically regular, had not been learned by phonic drill before being used in the sentences. **Dogs,** you may recall, had been included in sentence D-6 only at the children's request (page 119), and **bird** had been fitted to the end of D-16, a sentence composed mostly of tent words (page 128)—although **bird** itself had not been learned on the tents.

From all this, it seemed clear that words must be learned separately and well before they are employed in sentences, and that if they are learned as whole words, rather than as combinations of letter sounds their learning will be relatively slow even when a game is used to increase exposure and recall of them.

THE 50TH DAY—SUNDAY

All material except the *Red Hen* sentences was reviewed today.

When playing blocks, the children—Eve in particular—often sat facing the middle of the board (position X in *Fig. 19*), reading the words sideways, if not upside down.

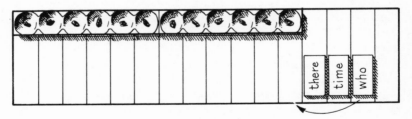

Fig. 19

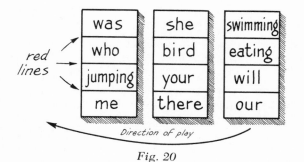

Fig. 20

This spot did, in fact, let the girls reach the blocks more easily, especially during the second half of the game. To induce right-way reading, the words were now printed breadthwise across the blocks (*Fig. 20*). The less useful of the *Red Hen* words—such as **grains, once,** and **upon**—were dropped from the game, and words needed for the new set of flip-flop sentences were added: **your, bird,** and **jumping.**

Each child read, in her turn, the twelve words, then moved the right-hand block in a jump left over the other two blocks and read the twelve words again before collecting a reward. In this way, the girls each read twenty-four words every turn. The game before supper progressed very slowly, as did the first part of the game after supper. Then, on receiving a particularly warm word of praise for a small accomplishment, Eve's voice rose in loudness and her reading accuracy reached a new peak.

The children sometimes became so excited while playing blocks that they had to work off their energy between turns. They did this by climbing over me or by tumbling on the couch or by sliding down the curved table legs. The girls howled for a second game; I granted them half a game. Both children continued to hesitate, fumble, and sound the letters of **will** before reading it, and by the end of the game Jean had forgotten **who**—a depressing note to end on.

THE 51ST DAY

Blocks proceeded so well this morning that a fourth block bearing the words **old, that, dog, skipping** was added halfway through the game, though, for the moment, only the word **old** was actually employed in the game. The 17 D sentences were then read, easily by Jean and better than usual by Eve, who this time hesitated less over the capital letters.

A paper bearing the letters **Bb, Mm, Dd, Aa** was clamped to the sun visor. Eve suggested the letters might be affixed to the top of the front seat to let her and Jean read them more easily from the back seat. An excellent idea!

I glued pieces of different-colored paper to each position on the blocks board in a manner that presented a pleasing rainbow effect. On seeing the decoration, Jean stated flatly she didn't like it (but reversed her opinion ten minutes later). The game began, and when the children had advanced the blocks a couple of positions along the board the word **that** (on the fourth block) was introduced. The girls asked permission to include in the game the other two words printed on that same block, **dog** and **skipping,** and were allowed to do so.

Until now, the children had always read words on each block from the bottom up. When, for the second game, Eve and Jean were asked to read the words from top to bottom instead, it became apparent that the girls had, to some extent, memorized the word sequence on each block, for it now took them twice as long to read the words.

At our later session, the blocks were drawn close together (as shown in *Fig. 21*), and the children were asked to read the words from left to right beginning at the top—**was, swimming, she, old**—and continue in this way down the four blocks. Alignment of the red lines helped the girls track the words easily across the blocks.

The use of four blocks raised the efficiency of the game to a new pinnacle. During each turn, the children read sixteen words twice, yielding thirty-two readings. After blocks, the girls asked to read the fifty-three sentences (twenty-six- + seventeen D + ten E). While reading, Eve confided to me that **B** was a kind of **b,** and **G** a kind of **g.**

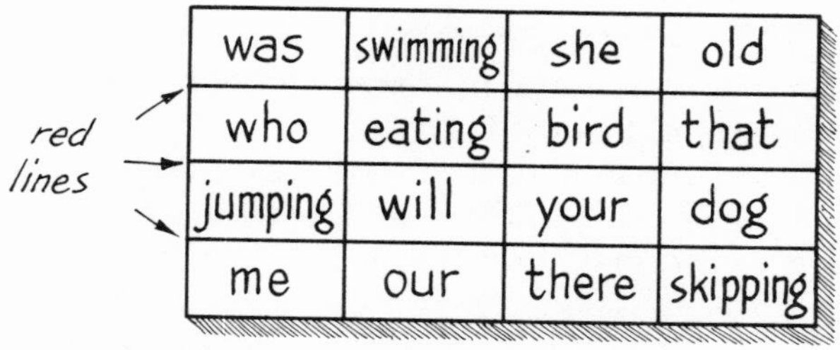

was	swimming	she	old
who	eating	bird	that
jumping	will	your	dog
me	our	there	skipping

red lines →

Fig. 21

THE 52ND DAY

The children continued to read the words on the blocks hesitantly as a result of the new horizontal-reading requirement. Because the order of words changed with every move, the girls couldn't memorize sequences. For example, the top four words at one moment—**swimming, was, she, old**—changed to **old, swimming, was, she** when the right-hand block was moved left. Eve requested an audience while reading, so a doll and a stuffed dog were propped up at her elbow. During the last part of the game a new block was introduced bearing the words **baby** and **singing**.

Acting on Eve's suggestion, I fastened a strip of cardboard to the back of the front seat in the car showing **dD, gG, eE, aA, tT, mM, hH, bB, fF, lL, rR.**

Until now, the smallest type face Eve has read was ¼ inch high. Jean, on the other hand, has read type just $5/32$ inch high in *The Little Red Hen* book. Could the children possibly read $3/32$-inch typewritten text now? This afternoon I typed three familiar sentences and with high hopes asked Eve if she could read them. She *could*—all three. Young Jean, by far the better reader, was slighted because I hadn't asked *her* if she could read them. So she was invited to try too.

The game of blocks before supper proceeded so smoothly that the words **elephant** and **running** were added. After bathing the children, I typed the three sentence lists—a total of fifty-three sentences (the twenty-six, seventeen D, and ten E), and the girls read them easily, though the sudden appearance of serifs created minor confusion with some letters.

THE 53RD DAY

There were no problems in reading the fifty-three sentences this morning, however, Eve was slow and easily distracted. I finally threatened to stop the exercise unless she concentrated on reading. This device invariably prompts greater effort while elevating the lessons to the status of a privilege.

A new block bearing the words **likes, hopping, has been, sitting** was included in the game. Strangely enough, Eve had difficulty identifying **likes** though she has read the word in the three 'like' sentences D-4, D-5, and D-6 (page 119) for weeks. The same material was reviewed during the afternoon and evening sessions.

THE 54TH DAY

The children were now able to read the content of six blocks (a total of twenty-four words). Three of the blocks were used for the first game this morning; the other three for the second. The girls then read the fifty-three sentences. Eve took much longer than Jean because every time she made an error (which was often), she glanced up smiling and lost her place, necessitating a ten-second search for the spot again.

There was just enough time left to introduce two more words—**dancing, monster**—on a new block and play four positions of the game. The children begged to know the other two words already printed on the same block, so I helped them sound out the letters in **wasn't** and **flying**, then lettered the words on a piece of paper for display in the car.

Tonight four more new words were introduced and learned—**sister, sleeping, Daddy, shopping.** The girls had now learned enough of the new sentence parts (listed on page 135) to begin composing and reading the new series of sentences in the flip-flop reader. But when I opened the reader, the children weren't able to recognize words in the body of a sentence they had recognized individually dozens of times when playing blocks!

THE 55TH DAY

Each of the eight word blocks now in use was included briefly in the game this morning for a review of the total thirty-two words they contain, then the children read the twenty-seven sentences (seventeen D + ten E, hereafter called the DE sentences). Strangely, Eve began having difficulty reading **trees**, and both children were puzzled by other old familiar words—**that, dog, eating**—in the new flip-flop sentences. It seems that words have to be learned in two separate ways—singly and again in the body of a sentence.

To quicken the children's recognition of upper-case letters, the words **JEAN, HAND, FROG, LAMB, TRIP** were printed then posted in the car.

I showed the children a list of the old twenty-six sentences this afternoon, typewritten entirely in capital letters, and held my breath. The girls read the sentences haltingly but with nowhere near the difficulty I had expected.

All eight blocks were reviewed before and after supper, and the last of the new composite sentence words—**isn't, hiding, crying**—were included in the game. Jean's reading of the flip-flop sentences was markedly improved, but Eve continued to flounder.

Now that the children could read typewritten text, their sentence lists could be altered quickly. I retyped the twenty-seven DE sentences, and rearranged their parts—for example, **This is the wrong street** was altered to **I went on the wrong street; Will we have jelly now?** became **Will we have carrots now?** Words in all the other sentences were similarly exchanged.

To help the children identify the new sentence parts in the flip-flop reader, the following fourteen sentences were composed and typed:

F-1.   A red bird has been swimming.
F-2.   Your black cat is skipping.
F-3.   Our big dog likes eating.
F-4.   That old hen was jumping.
F-5.   The baby pig isn't singing.
F-6.   This fat bear wasn't running.

F-7.   My little dolly will be hopping.
F-8.   The tall monster has been dancing.
F-9.   The elephant is flying.
F-10. My sister likes sleeping.
F-11. Daddy was hiding.
F-12. Who is crying?
F-13. Eve is sitting.
F-14. Jean likes shopping.

THE 56TH DAY—SATURDAY

Jean struggled through a reading of the new F sentences this morning. Neither child wanted to tackle the revised twenty-seven DE sentences.

The children's continuing puzzlement made me realize that I had advanced too quickly by presenting both *fresh* material (the F sentences) and *revised* material (the DE sentences), so I retyped the twenty-seven DE sentences in their original form (page 132) but with a sentence from the F list (above) substituted for every fifth sentence. The resultant list provided a succession of four easy-to-read sentences, then a difficult one. In this way, sentences F-1 to F-5 were presented to the children in a nondiscouraging manner, and during the two later sessions today the girls read the list easily. We reached a zenith of efficiency with the blocks: the game ended with all nine blocks (thirty-five words) in use simultaneously, each child reading *seventy* words every turn!

THE 57TH DAY—SUNDAY

The list of twenty-seven DE sentences was typed again, and five more F sentences (F-6 to F-10) were substituted for another five of the DE sentences. The children's reading of the resultant new list was generally good, though Eve, ever the puzzler, was stumped by words that she had read hundreds of times. Both girls had difficulty distinguishing between **That, The,** and **This,** but when I coached them in sounding the word parts—**th** being a voiced sound with the tongue fitting snugly between the teeth—their discrimination of the words improved.

There seemed to be little point in playing blocks with individual words when it was words within sentences that perplexed the girls. It was only a matter of time before I realized that if the blocks could produce a quick learning of words, they could probably produce a quick learning of sentences too. I immediately typed a different F sentence on three separate cards, affixed them to blocks, and assembled my class of two. Sure enough, after a few minutes of play, the children were able to read the sentences easily; and when two more F sentences—on a fourth and fifth block—had been learned quickly in this way, the problem seemed to be solved.

Fig. 22. A sentence block.

Eve wanted to play a second game; Jean didn't, but soon changed her mind when she saw the liberal way rewards were being heaped in the eggcups. The girls learned the first five F sentences so well that another five were added for the six-o'clock lesson. When that later session ended, five blocks were in play, two sentences per block, and the children were reading *twenty sentences every turn.*

The girls requested one more game of blocks before going to bed, but I'd had my fill; however, I relented and let each child have just one turn reading the ten sentences twice.

THE 58TH DAY

The children quickly learned the last four of the fourteen F sentences this morning. Later in the day, Eve caught her finger in a heavy fire door at the nursery. Miraculously, the finger remained intact, but she was in poor spirits most of the evening and, strangely, complained of a sore stomach. Jean alone read flip-flop sentences, then read the revised DE sentences she had spurned on Saturday.

THE 59TH DAY

The revised twenty-seven DE sentences and the fourteen F sentences had now all been typed on cards that could be quickly attached to or removed from blocks, thus providing a new collection of forty-one sentences the children can read. They reviewed twenty-two of these this morning. Eve's performance defied rational explanation, for she muffed **very, the,** and **Bring.**

Eve had an upset stomach again tonight. Jean alone played blocks before and after supper. I changed the cards frequently and she read thirty different sentences twice each. The twenty-seven revised DE sentences had been typed again, but this time in capital letters, and Jean read half the list.

THE 60TH DAY

We awoke late and had time for only fifteen minutes of play. Word cards replaced sentence cards on the blocks, and by using six blocks in the game, twenty-four words were reviewed.

Eve, ill again at the nursery today, was weak and sleepy tonight. Jean wanted to read flip-flop sentences and, with her sister looking on, read twenty-five newly composed sentences, played blocks with the word cards that hadn't been employed in the morning session, and ended by reading the list of twenty-seven revised DE sentences in capital letters.

There is, of course, no single moment when a child becomes a reader. Reading performance can't be measured in the precise manner of an athletic event. The children's reading ability, though admittedly imperfect, was now secure, and with no further instruction, their reading skill could be expected to improve during the two and three years before they entered grade 1. However, you may recall that my goal was not merely to teach the children to read, but to read well enough so they could enjoy children's books. How we accomplished that final task is the subject of the next chapter.

Several words that the children read only in simplified spelling have been omitted from this list, as have all *Red Hen* words that only one child could identify out of text.

a	did	hop	pants	sun
across	dinner	hopping	peg	supper
am	do	hot	pen	swimming
apples	dog		pet	
	dolly	I	pick	tall
baby		ill	pig	tea
back	eating	in	pin	ten
bag	eggs	is	pot	tell
banana	Eve	isn't	puppy	tennis
be	elephant	it	pumpkin	that
bear				the
been	fast	Jean	ran	there
beets	fat	jelly	rat	this
best	feels	jumping	red	time
big	feet	leg	ring	to
bird	fish	let	rub	today
biscuits	flying	like	rug	toilet
black	fog	lip	run	top
boots	for	little	running	trees
bread	free	lived		trick
breakfast	frog	long	scab	trip
bring	fun		see	truck
bug		lots	she	tub
bus	gas	lunch	shopping	
	get		sick	up
can	give	man	singing	
cap	grass	mat	sip	very
carrots	green	may	sister	
cat		me	sitting	want
clap	happy	met	skipping	was
clock	has	monster	sleeping	wasn't
cob	hat	morning	slip	we
corn	have	my	sock	well
could	help		soon	went
crib	hen	nap	step	wet
crying	here	not	stew	where
cub	hiding	now	stop	who
cup	hills		street	will
	him	of	string	win
Daddy	his	old	strong	would
dancing	hog	on		wrong
		our		

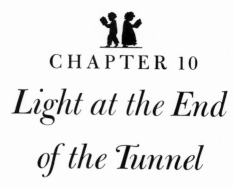

CHAPTER 10

Light at the End
of the Tunnel

61ST TO THE 76TH DAY

The children learned sixty-eight new words in the following
order in blocks during this period (two days of which were
lost due to illness).

1	2	3	4
teacher	near	behind	nice
girl	building	short	first
house	person	nurse	white
car	kitchen	blue	two
policeman	ceiling	farmer	nobody
by	standing	what	couldn't
are	between	air	can't
boat	someone	clown	laughing
beside	doctor	lady	along
road	under	outside	inside
corner	window	horse	musn't
around	chair	needs	won't
man	school	must	shouldn't
boy	above	cow	watching
small	train	one	wouldn't
floor	should	which	shouting
with	thing	duck	through

All earlier sentences, both composites and lists, were gradually eliminated as they were learned. A new series of composites (called the "silly" sentences), using the sixty-eight
words, were printed in the flip-flop reader in the following
manner.

page 1	The policeman	will be swimming	in his car.
	The teacher	likes skipping	by the boat.
	The girl	isn't eating	in the house.
page 2	My sister	has been jumping	on the road.
	The man	was singing	beside the house.
	A tall monster	is running	around the corner.
page 3	The small boy	wasn't hopping	on the floor.
	That person	is dancing	in our kitchen.
	Someone	will be flying	with the old pig.
page 4	The doctor	has been sleeping	near that building.
	That black thing	likes hiding	between the houses.
	The short man	isn't crying	on this ceiling.
page 5	A blue bird	wasn't sitting	at this school.
	The nurse	was shopping	on that chair.
	The fat clown	has been standing	under these windows.
page 6	The old farmer	should sit	in that train.
	The lady	must sing	above the floor.
	What	needs to dance	behind that tree.
page 7	Which frog	couldn't sit	outside the house.
	Which one	is laughing	in the air.
	That horse	can't swim	between the two buildings.
page 8	The cow	mustn't dance	in the white house.
	A small duck	won't jump	in the hospital.
	Nobody	is watching	along the floor.
page 9	The first hen	shouldn't jump	inside this train.
	That nice lady	has been shouting	through these windows.
		wouldn't eat	

Typing in the exercise book was not possible, of course, so
all the sentence parts had to be hand-lettered. There were
nine pages in all, with three complete sentences per page
(*Fig. 23*). Though this layout didn't permit intermatching of

The policeman	will be swimming	in his car.
The teacher	likes skipping	by the boat.
The girl	isn't eating	in the house.

Fig. 23

all the parts, more than two thousand different sentences could be composed, and the amusing surprises rising out of the unrelated parts helped to maintain the children's interest.

Eve and Jean were now confusing **b, d,** and **p,** so I purchased a small set of children's rubber stamps and stamped a picture of a boy on the backs of the children's right hands and a picture of a dog on the backs of their left hands (*Fig. 24*). Because the children normally read while resting on their hands and knees with the text situated midway between their hands, the stamped pictures would be positioned immediately to the right and left of the material being read.

Fig. 24

The girls were told that when the bulbous part of the letter "pointed" to the picture of the boy (on their right hand), the letter was **b** for *boy*, but if the "bump" pointed to the dog, on the left, the letter was **d** for *dog*. If, however, the letter had a "pretty" descending tail, then it was **p** for *pretty*. (The girls hadn't yet been introduced to **q**.)

The letters **b**, **d**, and **p** were then printed three quarters of an inch high several times in a mixed order on a sheet of paper (*Fig. 25*), and the children were asked to identify all twelve. They soon developed a chant for this: "This is a **p**, it has a pretty tail; this is a **b**, it points to a boy, no pretty tail"; and so on.

During this sixteen-day period, the children learned the first five sentences in a simple story book, *The Lion and the Deer*,[1] and added the words **deer, left, cave, hungry,** and **lion** to their reading vocabularies.

A major upset to our program occurred during this period (November 1, to be exact), when I accepted a full-time writing job. Unfortunately, there was no promise of permanency, so I couldn't drop my art clients who, alas, began loading me with work. Weekdays were therefore spent at an office, eve-

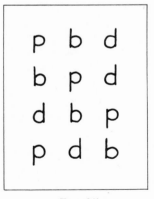

Fig. 25

1. Mention of this and other books should not be interpreted as a recommendation for their use. The selection of suitable books is covered in Chapter 12, page 193.

nings and week ends at home at my drawing board. The reading program seemed even more burdensome. In addition, I was now eager to know what the experts had to say about teaching children to read, and was reading pedagogical books at every spare moment.

Because of my new job, we had to leave the apartment an hour earlier each day. Morning sessions were no longer possible; nor were lessons before supper. And small chores that had formerly been done in odd moments throughout the day now awaited me when I returned home. To guarantee the children's close attention during the few moments left for reading instruction, some particularly powerful mood-bending rewards were introduced: peanut butter heaped on squares of bread or slices of banana, and topped with a raisin, peanut, or dot of jam. Slices of apple were used, as were morsels of sweet Chinese apricots, cream-filled biscuits (doled out in quarters), and even segments of canned pineapple rings.

77TH TO THE 95TH DAY

A figure 36 inches high was drawn on poster paper and attached to the wall (*Fig. 26*). Names for twenty-six parts of the body were printed on separate slips of colored paper and the children took turns sticking them to the appropriate parts of the drawing. When all the slips were attached properly, the girls read the names of body parts from a separate list and removed the appropriate slip from the drawing.

The girls found the game exciting but committed some amazing errors. For example, when searching for the **ankle** slip on the drawing, they looked everywhere on the figure except on the ankles. Although the poster improved the décor, it proved to be a slow vehicle for learning and was abandoned after only three days of use.

One day I noticed that Eve didn't point to the words she was reading. Acting on this sign, I began discouraging the use of fingers.

The children learned the following words by playing blocks, but with new rules that yielded a surprise:

Fig. 26

several	seven	field	lake
people	few	mountain	circus
some	couple	bridge	pond
three	many	sky	basement
four	five	cloud	ship
children	six	barn	store

Words were learned six at a time (two words on each of three blocks). Rewards in the first four eggcups were increased, but the children were now obliged to advance a second block for yet a *third* reading of the words in the one turn. In addition, the children were often asked to read the blocks still again (at extra payment) for any one of a number of reasons: slowness, hesitation, pointing, or simply as a challenge to them to see if they could read all the words correctly twice running.

Consequently, each child read the new words as many as twenty-four times in a single game lasting thirteen minutes, and by doing so, learned six words in a mere six-and-a-half minutes of participation. By this high-speed method, the children quickly learned all the new words needed for still another series of silly sentences:

page 1	Some nice elephants	couldn't swim	under the bridge at my school.
	These tall people	want to dance	near that mountain.
page 2	Little children	should sing	across that field.
	Several small dogs	wouldn't eat	in a tree outside this barn.
page 3	These four fat cats	could be standing	above these clouds.
	Three black cows	haven't been jumping	in the sky.
page 4	Five persons	won't run	with a clown at the circus.
	A couple of big blue fish	musn't laugh	beside this lake.
page 5	A few pigs	shouldn't dance	around the pond.
	Six black birds	will be hiding	behind that store.
page 6	Seven short monsters	have been flying	in our apartment.
	Many old bears	are sleeping	between these ships.

Components of the upper sentence on each page could not, of course, match components of the lower sentence. Still, 216 different sentences could be formed.

Reading of *The Lion and the Deer* (containing just twenty-two pages and averaging one sentence per page) proceeded at an extremely slow rate. We took six weeks to complete the book. Suddenly I realized how we might have finished the story in just a day or two. Indeed, by this new method the children read their second book, *Hooray for Henry*, in a single day, a Sunday.

First, I scanned the book and listed any words the children hadn't met before—there were twenty-four. By playing blocks, the girls learned the first twelve new words that appeared in the book, then read the first part of the book. Eve and Jean then learned the other twelve new words in the same way, and by bedtime, finished reading *Hooray for Henry*.

The advantages of mastering the phonic code had become increasingly evident. Jean, now an expert decoder, read many new words without help, among them **nurse, someone, nose, ear, hair,**[2] **peanut, water.** Moreover, skill with the code is influencing the children's speech, seen by their improved enunciation while reading, compared to their enunciation

---

2. Jean had already encountered the **ai** diphthong in *The Lion and the Deer* in the words **wait, waited,** and **said** (which she usually pronounced *sade*).

while talking, a refinement that can only be attributed to the girls' acute awareness of, and alertness to, individual letter sounds.

96TH TO THE 120TH DAY

I felt as if an oppressive weight had been lifted from my shoulders the day young Lynn Rivett became monitor for the children's reading program. I had only to establish rough guidelines for her to follow, then keep the plate of rewards well stocked. The blocks were no longer used. Instead, Lynn helped the children to sound new words as they were encountered and had them repeat each sentence several times before reading further. In this way, the children read their third book, *Barney Beagle*, in six days, and reviewed the first two books and composite sentences as well.

The one lesson with Lynn each day averaged an hour and a half. More time was possible on the week ends, though this, in part, only compensated for time lost through colds, chicken pox, and other upsets in our timetable. One way or another, the girls now received about nine hours of reading instruction each week. Reading performance improved—especially Eve's, for she was now reading as skillfully as Jean.

The list of books read by the children grew steadily longer, eventually including *One Kitten Is Not Too Many, The Little Red Hen, The Gingerbread Boy, Three Little Pigs,* and *The Birthday Party*.

The children sometimes sat on the floor at odd moments reading their books; and the sight of them doing so, brought sharply to mind the scene of 120 days earlier when in a similar pose, they had feigned a reading of the text to fit the accompanying illustrations.

Now with the sessions running smoothly under Lynn's good guidance, I discovered a bonanza. Not only was I released from the reading chore, but I was free from the children for one and a half hours every evening, free to get on with domestic or business matters without tripping over the girls or pausing to hear complaints, adjudicate claims, or referee their bickering.

During January, February, and March (fifth, sixth, and seventh months since our program began), in addition to rereading the first eight books several times, the children read fifteen new ones, increasing in difficulty up to *Red Riding Hood Also Goldilocks and the Three Bears, A Visit to the Doctor, Winnie-the-Pooh* (a simplified Disney version), as well as half a volume containing eleven relatively long tales, *Stories that Never Grow Old.*

As the children's skill advanced, it became obvious that their reading would soon be limited by their small speech vocabularies. Eve and Jean's situation was unusual in two ways. First, the girls rarely heard adult conversation, for, childish babble predominated at the nursery, and Eve and Jean's babble predominated in our apartment. Second, our television and radio sets were rarely switched on, so the girls didn't know many words that other three and four year olds took for granted.

To enrich the children's speech, fifty pictures, many from *National Geographic,* were attached to the walls, and name slips were affixed to any pictured item the girls didn't know by name. A reading of the slips became part of the regular lesson, and in this way, two hundred words were added to the children's speech vocabularies.

In April, the girls were shown how to read silently, and thereafter were periodically encouraged to practice this novelty. That same month, we began borrowing children's books from the public library. In fact, during the last two weeks of April, we hauled away sixty-seven books, of which the children read fifty-six plus six of their own.

Many of the books were, of course, quite simple, but you will recall that my purpose was to let the children enjoy the world of children's literature, not to equip them with an educational tool—though this latter function would be an ultimate fringe benefit.[3] Through May and June, the children

3. November, 1974: Eve and Jean, now six and five, have begun filling gaps in *my* education from their readings of the Britannica Junior Encyclopaedia before bedtime.

read fifteen to twenty books a week. Some were read for the first time; others were reread. A few were read at the nursery, some were read while waiting for supper, but most were read in bed; and though their cribs were just two feet apart, the girls read aloud from different books, oblivious of one another.

The reading skill, achieved painstakingly through the use of reward, now became a reward itself. For example, reading in bed before the light was turned out became a special favor earned by prompt, thorough brushing of teeth. And thereafter, whenever and wherever possible, the children were made to feel that the reading of books was an honor and privilege.

It is entirely possible, of course, that because of the children's unique conditioning, they may in future, on opening a new book, imagine the faint but unmistakable whiff of peanut butter or banana instead of printer's ink. If so, the phrases "reading taste" and "a book you can get your teeth into" will forever have uncommon significance for Eve and Jean.

PART 3

CHAPTER 11

Your Child's First 42 Sentences

From your child's standpoint, this is probably the most important chapter in the book. After you have read it one or more times, you will probably know instinctively how to handle any teaching problem that may arise. Even at this moment you know infinitely more about reading instruction than I did at the beginning of our program. Lack of firsthand experience in reading instruction can be an advantage, because you won't have preconceptions that might conflict with the program now to be presented.

The materials you will need for your reading program are listed on page 196. Circumstances will vary from home to home; in one, the mother will teach; in another, the father will; and in a third, both will teach. Both parents may work, or there may be only one parent.

Rather than try to accommodate these many possibilities, my remarks will be addressed to an imaginary Mrs. Average. I will assume that you, Mrs. A, though holding a regular job, will be teaching your three-year-old daughter Janice to read in a brief morning session (while Mr. A, makes the beds and gets breakfast ready), in a longer evening session (while Mr. A prepares supper), and perhaps even in a short session just before Janice goes to bed.

You may, of course, want to proceed at a more leisurely pace by having only one session each day. In this case, your child's progress, though slower, will be no less certain.

Select a spot for your lessons where Janice can be the center of attention and perhaps where father can glance over occasionally to beam approval at her triumphs. Disrupt the setting in some way that will remind the child to ask you to play the games or "school." If the focal object is silly, so much the better, for it will convey the message "fun thing going on here." For example, a couple of stuffed animals or dolls could be sitting in a colorful plastic bowl, waiting for the next "show" or "class" to start.

THE REWARDS

Rewards must be small enough to permit many payments without filling the child. Save the most delectable rewards for those times when you need an inducement with greater motivating power. It goes without saying that rewards should consist of foods above and beyond a child's daily needs. A food item necessary for balanced nutrition should not be in contest at any time.

Should a child be rewarded for providing wrong answers? A child should be rewarded for *trying*, not for coming up with right answers. On the other hand, don't immediately offer a reward for a wrong answer. Lead the child around to the right answer by easy questions. Even if you have to provide the answer, make it look as though she really knew the answer but couldn't think of it! Generally, the best teacher-training program you could wish for is your child's reaction. If she pouts or loses interest, you'll know you've just made a mistake (or perhaps a series of them).

Employ stickers and charts if you choose, but remember that some additional novelties are wisely held in reserve for a time when the child's interest is distracted or low (but low for reasons other than health or tiredness, of course).

THE ELECTRONIC HAZARDS

The seductive attraction of television can jeopardize your reading program. In solving the problem, there are two particular pitfalls to avoid: don't make TV viewing a reward for the child's good performance in the reading lesson, for it would only debase reading to the "superior, more desirable" pastime of watching TV; [1] and if the child's TV viewing must be reduced to accommodate the reading program, don't let the child see the connection, for you would immediately establish in the child's mind that the reading program was a kind of punishment (restricted TV viewing).

TV sets, radios, and record players would best be left off during reading sessions. In fact, the session should take priority over everything else within reason (including phone calls from friends). Treat the lessons as very important occasions in the hope that your child will consider them important too.

PUPPETS

I never thought to use a puppet in our reading program until the fifty-seventh day—too late—and, by this oversight, missed a valuable teaching aid. Recently, I learned to my surprise that an old acquaintance had used not one, but two puppets to teach his three year old to read, and he heartily recommended the technique. One of his puppets was a modest, likable fellow, the second was a loud braggart who continually blundered. Between them, the puppets kept the reading sessions lively.

By establishing a puppet as a "pupil," an entirely new situation is created. The child becomes less a pupil and more a "teacher," a title she will work hard to justify. The puppet as a perennial dunce in your small class provides great opportu-

1. However, this rule might be reversed for a child who already reads. In one reported case, a child "paid off" in minutes of TV watching for minutes spent reading books ultimately became so absorbed in reading that he forgot to turn on the television set.

nity for repetition and an ever-ready source of amusement.[2] Consequently, the following instructions invite the use of a single puppet. Naturally, you may use more puppets, or indeed no puppet at all, as you wish.

CHANGES

Had I my present knowledge of reading instruction when we began our program, some different procedures would have been used. One change would have been to teach upper-case letters first instead of lower-case letters. This and other improvements are presented in the instructions that follow.

Learning the capitals first yields two benefits: your child will be able to put her new reading skill to practical use more quickly. The simplest reading material in the world at large is usually presented in capital letters as in **GAS, IN, OUT, FREE, STOP, UP, DOWN, EXIT, WET PAINT, DANGER, MEN WORKING,** and so on; moreover, brand names, company names, titles, headings, and headlines are often shown in capitals. The second benefit concerns the apparently common problem of confusing the lower-case letters **b, d, p, q.** As you will see later, confusion between these four letters can easily be avoided once the capitals have been learned.

LETTERING

Hand lettering—a necessity for the first part of your reading program—is probably a skill you have never had reason to develop. If so, practice making capital letters before starting the program. Use lined notepaper; the lines will provide ready guidelines to help you achieve a conformity of letter heights. Omit serifs from your letters; not only do serifs make printing more difficult, they confuse the basic letter shapes (*Fig. 27*).

2. Nothing tickles a child's fancy more than being able to crow over the ineptitudes of a silly person. Of all the books Eve and Jean have read, none delighted them more than *Amelia Bedelia,* the story of a dull-witted housemaid who always does everything wrong.

with serifs

JKL

JKL

without serifs

Fig. 27

PHONIC SOUNDS

Be precise in your interpretation of the letters as sounds. The consonant sounds that couple voice with a movement of the mouth—**B, D,** and **G**—must be sounded quickly. When sounding **B,** the voiced sound should stop abruptly as the lips part. For **D** and **G,** the voice should stop immediately when the tongue separates from the roof of the mouth.

Notice that all the following letters are *not* accompanied by a voiced sound, but are made solely by releasing air in different ways—**C** (as in *cat*), **F, H, K, P, T.** Note, too, the letters **L, M, N, R, S, U, V, W,** though sounding different from each other, represent in each case just a single, steady voiced sound, and must not end with a vowel sound—for example, **M-M-M,** not **M-M-Muh.**

GETTING STARTED

Begin the program on a day when you can have several short sessions at regularly spaced intervals—perhaps a Saturday, permitting you to hold additional short sessions on Sunday too. By Sunday night, everyone would probably be well adjusted to the new routine.

Prepare a reading area—perhaps with a puppet propped up in some way; a jar or dish of rewards; and this book, opened to page 198. You might arrange for Janice to discover the setting when she awakes Saturday morning, or you could simply put the materials out and ask her if she'd like to help you teach the puppet to read.

In the instructions that follow, no stopping and starting points for individual sessions have been indicated because each parent and child will determine by their progress, performance, and a host of other variables the best time and place to stop a lesson. As a rule—and it's a golden rule— always stop a session while your child wants to continue a little longer. By leaving a residue of enthusiasm you will leaven the child's interest for the next session. There is also a golden rule for starting a session—always begin by reviewing material so absurdly simple that your child couldn't possibly have forgotten it (or so you may think). Allowing the child a few initial triumphs helps generate an optimism that will permit her to deal confidently with newer, more difficult material.

Let's assume that you are ready now with the puppet on one hand, and that Janice, positioned for correct viewing of the letter **A,** is waiting for you to begin.

THE LETTER **A**

If Janice knows **A** is called a letter, fine—though this information in itself isn't important. In Janice's mind, a letter is more likely something that is dropped in a mailbox, and there is no need to explain the difference at this moment. Just tell the child (indirectly, by informing the puppet) that this funny shape tells us to make a certain sound. Demonstrate the sound (as in *bat,* but without mentioning the bat). If Janice says, "No, it's called *ay,*" agree that though the shape does have that name, there is a difference between the *name* of a letter and its *sound.* You might point out that though an animal is called a *cow,* it doesn't say *cow,* but *moo.* Similarly, the letter is called *ay,* but it tells us to make the **A** sound.[3]

---

3. Knowing the names of the letters (the traditional ABCs), though better than no knowledge of the alphabet at all, is of much less value than knowing the sound of the letters. Though Eve and Jean knew the ABCs from having sung the song at the nursery, they didn't use this information until after they had learned to read, when, in fact, they began learning to print and spell.

Try to get the puppet (let's call him Archie) to sound **A** properly. He falters and fails. Enlist Janice's help to teach him, and when she has made the sound properly several times, let the puppet finally say it correctly. Give Janice a reward for her good teaching, and as many rewards from now on as are justified by her responses and assistance.

Read aloud the story of Albert the alligator on page 199 of this book, or tell it in your own words, while moving the ambulance as described.

Ask the puppet the questions at the bottom of page 199. Don't direct your questions to Janice or indicate that you expect her to know the answers. If Janice knows any answer, she'll soon tell you. On the other hand, if you ask her a question directly and she doesn't know the answer, you unnecessarily make her feel uncomfortable.

Ask the puppet question 1. If Janice doesn't volunteer the information, tell the puppet the correct answer. Ask the puppet Question 2, and, in doing so, emphasize the beginning sound. If Janice doesn't respond, ask the puppet again, this time repeating the first letter as you would in a slow stutter, **a-a-a-alligator**. If Janice still doesn't respond (and this is to be expected), tell the puppet the answer. Follow the same procedure for questions 3, 4, 5, and 6.

Keep the exercise light and humorous. Let Archie make an idiot of himself. Whenever Janice is right, make a big fuss over her with hugs and rewards. Praise her to Archie and tell the puppet he will have to hurry up or be left behind. In actual fact, to fulfill his role most effectively, Archie must *always* be left behind, never knowing something Janice doesn't.

Begin all over again now. Start by telling the puppet what sound the shape tells us to make. Can he make the sound? Janice can perhaps be made as zealous as a missionary in trying to imprint this knowledge on the seemingly unteachable puppet's "brain." If so, good.

Repeat the story of Albert the alligator, omitting no detail, as if for the first telling. But this time, let Janice move the ambulance around the circuit (twice in the course of the story), and quiz the puppet again so Janice can demonstrate her superior memory.

Repeat the entire procedure a third time. Now, in addition to letting Janice move the ambulance, pause and let her supply key words in the story: "An alligator named —— was driving his ——" and so on. "Something broke. What was it? Yes, an axle." Continue to repeat the routine until Janice can answer the questions correctly.

Will Janice become familiar with the **A** sound the first session? She might. But *don't* introduce the next letter during the first session. A slow beginning helps assure quick progress later. Too fast a pace at the beginning invites confusion, and confusion slows learning. (You will recall that Eve and Jean were still occasionally confusing **a, b,** and **c** after a dozen sessions; this, the high cost of presenting new material before they had properly learned earlier material.) The expression "hurry ahead slowly" is worth applying to your entire program. Proceed no further until **A** has been well learned.

THE LETTER **C**

Introduce the letter **C** only after having thoroughly reviewed **A** first. **C** has been chosen for the second letter instead of **B** to minimize possible confusion (both **A** and **B** have upper and lower sections). Show the puppet the large **C** on page 200 and say that this shape tells us to make the sounds heard at the end of *tic;* but just make the sound without mentioning tic. Remember, this is not a voiced sound (see *Phonic sounds*, page 165).

When Archie, aided by your daughter, can make the sound correctly, read the story on page 200. Don't be afraid to enlarge upon details of the story.

Quiz the puppet, and when, with your daughter's help, he can answer all the questions sensibly, tell Archie the story again, with Janice filling in key words. Perhaps she would then like to tell the puppet the whole story herself and quiz him too. What better way to find out how well Janice has learned the material? The better a teacher Janice becomes, the better a pupil she will be. You might, therefore, wish to introduce a second puppet solely for the purpose of receiving

Janice's instruction. Your daughter may be inspired to teach at a highly competent level, especially if Archie "helps" by getting in his two cent's worth of wrong information.

When Janice has a good understanding of the letter **C,** review the letter **A** again. Don't introduce the letter **B** during that same session.

Just before showing the letter **B,** review **A** and **C** again. Let Archie see the **B** on page 201, and demonstrate the sound it represents at the end of *tub;* but just make the sound without mentioning the tub. Keep the sound short, as described on page 165. When he is able, with Janice's help, to make the sound, tell him the story on page 201 and ask him the questions.

Repeat the story until the puppet can provide the correct answers. If, occasionally, he is so dull that Janice becomes exasperated, you will probably develop an eager teaching ally with whom you can then plot the puppet's rise to literacy.

When Janice can easily distinguish among **A, B,** and **C,** open the book to expose **A** (page 198) and, moving the letter away from her gradually to a distance of 10 feet, point out that **A** remains **A** regardless of its size. Leaving the book open at that distance show Janice, at a distance of 12 inches, a 1½-inch letter **A** affixed to a block. She will then see that the shapes are identical.

On showing Janice the letters **B** and **C** similarly affixed to blocks, you will then be ready for your first game of blocks (see page 196). Archie will participate, of course, and his absurd performance should fasten Janice's attention on the game.

Repeat the game until Janice develops an easy recognition of the three letters. At any sign of forgetfulness, go back over the exercise for that particular letter.

When—and only when—Janice has completed a game of blocks without making errors, turn to page 202 and introduce her to Sammy Snake. Can Archie make the hissing sound at the beginning of the word *snake?* That's the sound the letter **S** tells us to make. Now tell Janice the story.

When Janice has properly associated the **S** shape with the hissing sound, print an **S** and affix it to a block. After starting the game with the other three blocks, put **S,** the fourth block into play.

Janice is now ready to read her first three words: **BAC, CAB,** and **SCAB,**[4] but tell her you think the puppet is ready to read. Position the letters **B, A, C,** as shown, (*Fig. 28*) and ask Archie to sound the individual letters at an ever-increasing speed until he can hear the word *back* being spoken. He becomes hopelessly confused, of course, so Janice must show him how. When she has sounded the letters a few times, produce a slip of paper bearing the word **BAC** printed in letters of the same size, and have her sound the individual letters first, then the complete word (*Fig. 29*).

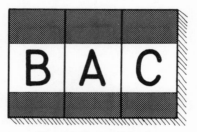

Fig. 28. Letter blocks.

Fig. 29. A word slip.

There is no reason why Janice should not pay the puppet rewards when he performs properly. In fact, she might find the paying of rewards as satisfying as receiving rewards. Of course, she will need be informed that puppets usually eat when they wake up in the middle of the night.

Repeat the entire procedure, first with the letter blocks, then with word slips, for **CAB** and **SCAB.** When Janice can

4. In those areas of America where a paper shopping bag is called a *sack,* a fourth word would be available in **SAC.**

sound these easily, have another game of blocks, but now with the blocks positioned horizontally and each bearing a word slip (*Fig. 30*). The procedure now and for every future word when playing blocks is to first sound the individual letters of a word, then sound the word itself.

Fig. 30. *Word blocks (blocks with word slips attached).*

Familiarize Janice with new letters plenty of time before you want to employ them. Letters will be introduced in the order they appear on the following pages. Spend a few minutes at the end of each session showing Janice the letter shapes and the drawings associated with each, then by the time you are ready to include the letters in the lessons, she will be familiar with them. Also, begin drawing attention to the beginning sounds of words at every opportunity, especially words beginning with sounds soon to be introduced.

Fig. 31

Three new words should be included in the game of blocks now: **I, YOU,** and **JANICE** (meaning, of course, your own child's name). Substitute **I** for one of the old blocks and have a game. The letter **I** will be sounded, of course, as in *bite*, not as in *bit*. Next, substitute **YOU** for another of the old blocks and have a second game. The word **YOU** is among that small group of words (about 15 per cent) that are not entirely consistent with the basic rules of the phonic code, therefore **YOU** should be spoken as a complete word without sounding its individual letters.

Finally, introduce **JANICE,** and have a game with the three new blocks (*Fig 31*). When your child is completely at ease with the three words, affix three new slips to the blocks, each slip bearing *two* words (*Fig. 32*), and have another game.

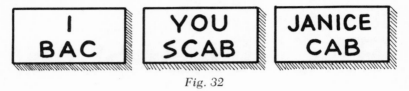

Fig. 32

When Janice feels comfortable with the smaller type size (which may take several games), prepare new slips for the blocks, now turned vertically again, with each slip sectioned in four, and with the six words printed in the upper two sections of the slips (*Fig. 33*). Play blocks until Janice has no trouble with this smaller type size.

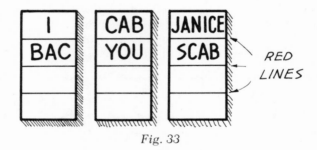

Fig. 33

If you haven't already acquainted Janice with the letter **U,** do so now, sounded as it is heard at the beginning of *umbrella,* then tell her the following story:

When Mr. Upside-down was caught in the rain one day, he rushed into a store and bought an umbrella—the first Mr. Upside-down had ever owned. And this is how he held the umbrella. What sound does the shape tell us to make? What sound does Upside-down begin with? Umbrella? Uncle?

Replace one of the blocks with one bearing the words **US,** and play the game. When Janice has learned **US,** replace the

Fig. 34. Mr. Upside-down.

slip with another bearing two words—**US** and **BUS.** After more play, substitute a slip bearing three words—**US, BUS,** and **CUB.** When all three words have been well learned, add them to the blank spaces on the earlier blocks. Then add **SUC** to a new block. Continue to add new words in this way, and when they have been learned, transfer them to the blank spaces on the other blocks. Occasionally, four blocks might be in play at once.

Of course, as each new letter is learned, many more words can be formed than the few that are presented, and the natural desire is to want to quickly expand a child's reading vocabulary. But at this point, the more important task is to help Janice master the phonic key which will permit her to unlock not merely hundreds of words, but the entire English language. Therefore, resist the temptation to introduce easy-to-learn extra words.

As still more words are added to the game, older blocks can be removed, to be included again periodically for review. Learning the letter **T** permits the introduction—one at a time—of **TUB, CUT, SAT, CAT,** and **BUT** to the game. Show Janice the illustration (*Fig. 35*); explain that *tongue* begins

Fig. 35

with the **T** sound; and in front of a mirror, let her see this shape formed by her own tongue.

On introducing **EE** (for which no mnemonic key is provided), the words **SEE, BEE, BEET,** and **TEE** (for *tea*) can be included. In your lettering, make the bar of the first **E** touch the second **E,** as shown (*Fig. 36*). If Janice can be made to think of the double **E** as being one large complex shape rather than a combination of two **E**s she will not then have really met the proper **E** shape, and will not be puzzled later to learn the **E** usually represents the vowel sound heard in *bet*.

Fig. 36

The learning of **M** (just a humming sound, and *not* ending with a vowel sound) permits the introduction of **MEET** and **MAT.** Show Janice the illustration (*Fig. 37*). What other words besides *monkey* begin with the humming sound? An even more startling way of fixing the **M** sound in the child's mind would be to letter an **M** on your own forehead—**M** for *Mummy*. One last word to include in the game is **WEE** (for *we*). When Janice can sound the individual letters and voice the words easily, she is almost ready to begin reading sentences.

Fig. 37

Show Janice how, by placing an **A** in front of certain words, recognizable expressions are formed—**A TUB, A CAT, A BUS,** and so on. Repeat the exercise periodically. Bear in mind that this is a complicated function for a child to understand.

Next, show Janice how the addition of **S** to certain words forms the plurals—**BACS, CUTS, CATS, BEETS, MATS.** But don't add **S** to any word that requires the **S** to be buzzed (*tub, cub, scab,* and others).

These procedures, though extremely simple for you, are highly complex operations to a child. Therefore, puzzlement and uncertainty are the most natural and normal responses Janice could express. Show her you don't mind. And don't be too clinical. Hugging goes farther than detailed explanation in making the program a success.

THE FLIP-FLOP READER

Between sessions, prepare the following material. On the first page of a coil-wire-bound 8½-by-11-inch exercise book, rule light pencil lines, as shown in the illustration, to serve as guides for your lettering (*Fig. 38*). With a needle, pierce as many pages as you can near the ends of each line. Lift the top page, and, using the pinholes for reference, draw the same lines on the second page that you drew on the first page. Continue in this way until fourteen pages have been lined (*U* lines need be ruled only on the first five pages).

Slit the fourteen pages in the middle from the binding to the outer edge so that the left and right halves can move free-

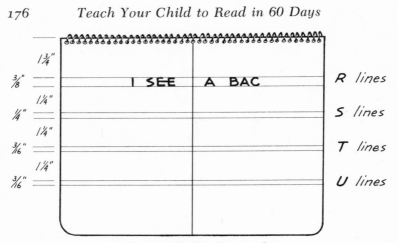

Fig. 38. The flip-flop reader.

ly and independently of each other. For the moment, we are concerned with lettering only between the *R* lines. On the first left-hand page, print **I SEE,** as shown. Lift that page and, between the *R* lines on the next page, print **YOU SEE.** In the same place on the next page under that, print **WEE SEE.** On the first right-hand page, print **A BAC,** as shown. Flip the page, and print **A CAB.** Continue to print the following sentence components on the right-hand pages on the *R* lines of successive pages: **A SCAB, A BUS, A CUB, A TUB, A CUT, CATS, A BEE, BEETS, A MAT, TEE, US, JANICE.**

Announce with considerable excitement that you think the puppet is ready to read his first sentences, and let Archie try to read **I SEE A BAC.** When he fails, let Janice try, and when she succeeds, begin changing the components by flipping pages. But change only a right-hand or left-hand page at a time, never both at once. Continue in this way each session until Janice can read the material easily.

The amount of hand lettering needed can be greatly reduced by teaching Janice to read small type early in the program, for she will then be able to read directly from this book, thus saving you the task of lettering sentences in larger characters.

When Janice is able to read the flip-flop material well (this may take another week or two), print the components again, but in ¼-inch-high letters between the S lines (rearranging the order, of course, so that the larger lettering on each page doesn't read the same as the smaller lettering). When, ultimately, Janice can read the smaller lettering easily, letter the material again between the ³⁄₁₆-inch T lines and repeat the exercises.

As her skill increases, Janice will begin reading words without troubling to sound out individual letters first. Encourage her to do this, but without making a big issue of it when she doesn't.

CHAPTER 12

The Final Enduring Gift

If Janice falters when reading a word, don't make a habit of reading the word for her. Instead, have her sound the letters with your help.

Rules are often more puzzling than helpful, so refer to rules of pronunciation as little as possible. A child should, of course, be told that the letters **C** and **H,** when joined, produce a new sound unlike either, and that the same occurs with **S** and **H, O** and **I, O** and **O** (though irregular), and one or two others, but rules shouldn't be harped on. Janice's reading experience will gradually provide her with the insight that rules are supposed to do.

In preparation for the addition of more sentence components to your flip-flop reader, rule *T* lines on twenty more pages and slit those pages. To simplify instructions for the printing of new words in the book, the terms *T-r, T-l, U-r, U-l*, will be used to indicate which line to print on, and whether it is a right- or left-hand page.

The **F** shape tells us to make the sound heard at the beginning of *flag (Fig. 39)*. This drawing will help establish the relationship in Janice's mind. When you have discussed other words that begin with **F,** teach the words **FEET, FAT,** and **MY** [1] by playing blocks, then add **MY FAT FEET** and **MY FAT CAT** to two pages of flip-flop reader *(T-r)*.

1. The letter **Y** can create confusion if one attempts a detailed explanation of its various sounds—as occurs in *you, my*, and *funny* (not to mention *myth*

Fig. 39

Explain that the letter **I** is often sounded another way, as in the word **IT,** and **S** is sometimes buzzed as in the word **IS.** Include **IT IS** in the game of blocks along with **BISCIT, SIC,** and **AM.**

Add **A BISCIT** to the reader (*T-r*), then begin a second set of composite sentences on the *U* lines by printing on the first two pages **IT IS, I AM** (*U-l*), and **SIC, FAT** (*U-r*).

Print the letter **H** on the back of Janice's hand at an angle that lets her view it correctly, and sound it for her—just air forced from the throat without voiced sound. What other words beside *hand* start with this sound?

Introduce the words **HAV** and **HAT.** Spend a moment coaching Janice on the sound of **V**—just a steady voiced sound with the upper teeth resting on the lower lip. Play blocks, and when **HAV** and **HAT** are learned, add **I HAV, YOU HAV** (*T-l*), and **A HAT** (*T-r*) to the slit-page reader.

Print the letter **O** and show Janice how your mouth assumes this shape when you sound it (as in *hop,* not *hope*). Add **SOC, HOT,** and **COB** to the blocks, and when these are easily read, print **A HOT COB** and **A SOC** in the reader (*T-r*).

Introduce the word **THIS,** explaining that the combination of **T** and **H** sounds unlike either of these letters separately. You might invent a little story about **T** marrying **H** (use sounds only, not names of the letters), and because **T** didn't want to sound like **H,** and **H** didn't want to sound like **T,** they agreed to call themselves **TH** (the voiced sound with the tongue positioned between the teeth).

Draw the letter **W** on a piece of paper and tell Janice that

---

and *myrrh*). For the moment, teach **MY** as being composed of two sounds, *m-m-m* and the sound of *eye*.

this wiggly line tells us to make the sound that *wiggly* begins with—just a voiced sound while the lips are pushed out to form a tiny circle.

Show Janice a used envelope blackened along two edges and tell her that this shape represents the same sound *letter* begins with (*Fig. 40*). Introduce **WIL, LITL, BLAC, IL, CLOC, LOTS, FEEL, MILC,** and **THIS** into a game of blocks, then eventually add to the flip-flop reader **I FEEL** (*U-l*), **IL** (*U-r*), **I WIL SEE, I WIL HAV, THIS IS** (*T-l*), **LOTS OF MILC** and **A LITL CLOC** (*T-r*). Janice may not even notice that **F** sounds like a **V** in the word **OF.** If she does notice, pass over the point lightly.

Fig. 40

As more components are added, some sentences that don't make sense will be formed. Perhaps the puppet could provide some humorous comment on these occasions.

Introduce Janice to the purple pickle-eater who lives in a paper bag (*Fig. 41*). Put **THE, PIC, UP, HAPY, PUPY, CUP** on blocks. Then add **THE BLAC PUPY, THE CUP OF MILC, THE HAPY CUB** to the reader (*T-r*).[2]

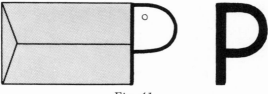

Fig. 41

2. Point out that the first two letters in the word **THE** sound the same as the first two letters in **THIS.** Don't emphasize the fact that the **E** in **THE** is not consistent with the phonic code. If, in sounding the individual letters of **HAPY** and **PUPY** for Janice, she notices that the letter **Y** has a different sound

Do you know what happened to an elephant named Edward who sprayed his trunk for moths? Well, the illustration shows him before and after, and in his reclining state he helps us link the beginning sound of *elephant* to **E** *(Fig. 42)*. Include **HELP, WEL,** and **MET** in the game of blocks, then print **HELP PIC UP, I MET** *(T-l)*, and **WEL** *(U-r)*.

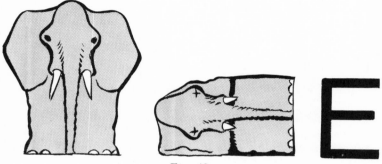

Fig. 42

Mr. Nelson's nose is as sharp as a needle *(Fig. 43)*. What other words begin with the sound this shape represents? Add **FUNY, STIF, CAN, MAN, NEC** to the blocks; then **CAN I HAV** *(T-l)*, **THE FUNY MAN, A STIF NEC** *(T-r)*.

Fig. 43

from when it appeared in the word **YOU,** simply tell her that's the way it is, and drop the matter. Children will usually accept phonic irregularities as being perfectly justified.

When the one-eyed gurb encounters something too horrible to see, it simply retracts its eye and mutters **G-G-G-G.** Here, then, are two ways the gurb might appear, depending on the view (*Fig. 44*). Incorporate the words **BIG, STIC, GUM, BAG, PIG** into a game of blocks, then add **A STIC OF GUM, THE FAT PIG, A BIG BAG** (*T-r*).

Fig. 44

Ronald Rabbit likes to run, run, run in the radish patch (*Fig. 45*). Play blocks with **STRONG, FROG, STREET, RONG, GREEN, WHERE,** then add **WHERE IS** (*T-l*), **THE GREEN FROG, THE RONG STREET** (*T-r*), and **STRONG** (*U-r*).

Fig. 45

Ducks and ducklings both start with the sound that **D** represents (*Fig. 46*). Play blocks with **DID, DOG, RED, THAT,** then add **DID YOU SEE** (*T-l*), **THAT GREEN DOG, THAT RED FROG** (*T-r*).

For **J,** show the drawing of this jet aircraft (*Fig. 47*). The sound and shape should then lodge securely in Janice's mind.

Fig. 46

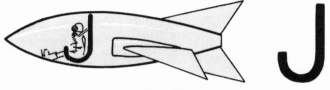

Fig. 47

All words that have been presented in simplified spelling are included in the following fourteen sentences. Coach Janice in reading them, either from the book or in enlarged hand lettering if she is not yet able to read small type face. Tell her that **K** represents the **C** sound both when it is combined with the letter **C** and when it is shown alone (as in *milk*). Double **E**s should no longer touch one another. Proceed no further in your reading program until Janice can read these sentences easily.

I HAVE A STIFF NECK

CAN I HAVE A CUP OF TEA

PICK UP THE BLACK PUPPY

THIS IS A STICK OF GUM

THIS IS THE WRONG STREET

THIS IS A SOCK

WE SEE A SICK CAT

I MET A FUNNY MAN

THIS IS A BISCUIT

I SEE A LITTLE CLOCK

I WILL HAVE LOTS OF MILK

I SEE A HAPPY CUB

MY BACK IS WELL

I FEEL ILL

When Janice has mastered all the material up to this point, measure fourteen more pages in your flip-flop reader as shown in the diagram (*Fig. 48*) and cut them so as to provide three independently movable sections of *A* (4½ inches), *B* (2 inches) and *C* (4½ inches).[3]

3. Though all fourteen pages won't be needed for the first group of sentences (*V*), they will be required for another group of sentences that will ultimately go on the *W* lines of the flip-flop reader.

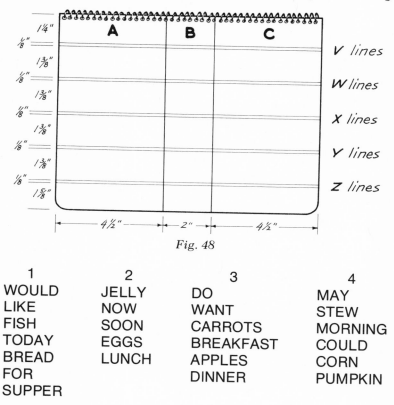

Fig. 48

1	2	3	4
WOULD	JELLY	DO	MAY
LIKE	NOW	WANT	STEW
FISH	SOON	CARROTS	MORNING
TODAY	EGGS	BREAKFAST	COULD
BREAD	LUNCH	APPLES	CORN
FOR		DINNER	PUMPKIN
SUPPER			

Play blocks with the first three words in column 1 above, and when they are learned, add another word on a fourth block. When it too is learned, print the words again, this time *two* to a block, and introduce still another new word on a third block. Continue in this way, adding new words from column 1 gradually to the game and printing them anew so that they all remain in the game but without ever using more than four blocks.

When the words in the first column are learned, print those sentence parts above the solid line (at V) on successive pages of the flip-flop reader on the V lines—**WOULD YOU LIKE** on the V lines of the first *A* page section, **WE WOULD LIKE** on the V lines of the second *A* section beneath that, and so on,

	A	B	C
V	WOULD YOU LIKE WE WOULD LIKE	FISH BREAD	TODAY FOR SUPPER
	WE WILL HAVE WILL WE HAVE CAN I HAVE	JELLY BEETS EGGS	NOW SOON FOR LUNCH
	DO YOU WANT I WANT	CARROTS APPLES	FOR BREAKFAST FOR DINNER
	MAY I HAVE COULD I HAVE	STEW CORN PUMPKIN	THIS MORNING

with the five sentence beginnings being entered on the *V* lines of the first five *A* sections.

Similarly, print **FISH** and **BREAD** on the *V* lines of the first and second *B* page sections. Print **TODAY** and **FOR SUPPER** on the *V* lines of the first and second *C* page sections.

With five beginnings, two middles, and two endings, you will now be able to compose a total of twenty different sentences. When Janice is able to read these easily—perhaps in a week or so—teach her the words in column 2 by playing blocks, then add the sentence parts above the line of dashes at *V* to the *V* lines on appropriate pages of the flip-flop reader. One hundred and twenty-five sentences may now be composed and practiced. Later, teach the words in column 3, and add the sentence parts above the dotted line to the reader. Finally, teaching the words in column 4 will permit the inclusion of the remaining sentence parts in the reader.

Repeat the entire procedure with the following words, and print the sentence components listed at *W* on the *W* lines in the flip-flop reader.[4]

4. In the word **DANCING**, Janice will see, for the first time, the letter **C** sounded as a hiss. Simply tell her this change sometimes occurs, and that she will soon learn to tell whether a **C** should be sounded like a **K** or an **S**. Even this much explanation may not be necessary.

1	2	3	4
BIRD	OLD	BEAR	ELEPHANT
HAS	HEN	WASN'T	FLYING
BEEN	WAS	RUNNING	SISTER
SWIMMING	JUMPING	DOLLY	SLEEPING
YOUR	BABY	BE	DADDY
SKIPPING	ISN'T	HOPPING	CRYING
OUR	SINGING	TALL	WHO
EATING		MONSTER	HIDING
		DANCING	SITTING
			SHOPPING

A	B	C
A RED BIRD	HAS BEEN	SWIMMING
YOUR BLACK CAT	IS	SKIPPING
OUR BIG DOG	LIKES	EATING
THAT OLD HEN	WAS	JUMPING
THE BABY PIG	ISN'T	SINGING
THIS FAT BEAR	WASN'T	RUNNING
MY LITTLE DOLLY	WILL BE	HOPPING
THE TALL MONSTER		DANCING
THE ELEPHANT		FLYING
MY SISTER		SLEEPING
DADDY		CRYING
MUMMY		HIDING
WHO		SITTING
		SHOPPING

W

LEARNING THE LOWER-CASE LETTERS

Explain to Janice that there is another way to make the letter **D,** and let her read the following **d** sentences:

1
A REd BIRd HAS BEEN dANCING
THE TALL MONSTER WASN'T JUMPING
d THIS FAT BEAR WILL BE SLEEPING
OUR BIG dOG LIKES SINGING
THE BABY PIG ISN'T FLYING
YOUR BLACK CAT WAS HIdING

The next day, explain there is another way to make **A**s, and let Janice read the following **a** sentence list:

2
a REd BIRd HaS BEEN daNCING
THE TaLL MONSTER WaSN'T JUMPING
a THIS FaT BEaR WILL BE SLEEPING
OUR BIG dOG LIKES SINGING
THE BaBY PIG ISN'T FLYING
YOUR BLaCK CaT WaS HIdING

Continue in this way, showing another lower-case letter each day, and have Janice read the list that includes the new letter form. Lower-case letters that closely resemble their upper-case counterparts should present no problem to Janice and need not be emphasized.

For each day this exercise is in progress, show the letters **J, I, H, L,** and **B,** printed in 3-inch-high letters. Hide part of each letter (*Fig. 49*) and ask Janice to sound it. This procedure will take on the spirit of a joke, for she will, of course, spy the letter before you hide a portion of it.

Fig. 49

3

a REd BIRd HaS BEEn danCInG
THE TaLL MOnSTER WaSn'T JUMPInG
THIS FaT BEaR WILL BE SLEEPInG
OUR BIG dOG LIKeS SInGInG
THE BaBY PIG ISn'T FLYInG
YOUR BLaCK CaT WaS HIdInG

n

4

a rEd BIrd HaS BEEn danCInG
THE TaLL MOnSTEr WaSn'T JUMPInG
THIS FaT BEar WILL BE SLEEPInG
OUr BIG dOG LIKES SInGInG
THE BaBY PIG ISn'T FLYInG
YOUr BLaCK CaT WaS HIdInG

r

5

a red BIrd HaS Been danCInG
THe TaLL MOnsTer WaSn'T JUMPInG
THIS FaT Bear WILL Be SLeePInG
OUr BIG dOG LIKeS SInGInG
THe BaBY PIG ISn'T FLYInG
YOUr BLaCK CaT WaS HIdInG

e

6

a red BIrd Has Been danCInG
THe TaLL MOnsTer Wasn'T JUMPInG
THIs faT Bear WILL Be sLeePInG
OUr BIG dOG LIKes sInGInG
THe BaBY PIG Isn'T fLYInG
YOUr BLaCK CaT Was HIdInG

f (s)

7

a red BIrd Has Been dancIng
THe TaLL MOnsTer Wasn'T JUMPIng
THIs faT Bear WILL Be sLeePIng
OUr BIg dOg LIKes slngIng
THe BaBY PIg Isn'T fLYIng
YOUr BLacK caT Was HIdIng

g (c)

8

a red BIrd Has Been dancIng
THe TaLL monsTer Wasn'T JumPIng
THIs faT Bear WILL Be sLeePIng
our BIg dog LIKes slngIng
THe BaBY PIg Isn'T fLYIng
Your BLacK caT Was HIdIng

m (o, u)

9

t (p, w, y)

a red BIrd Has Been dancIng
tHe taLL monster wasn't JumpIng
tHIs fat Bear wiLL Be sLeepIng
our BIg dog LIKes sIngIng
tHe BaBy pIg Isn't fLyIng
your BLacK cat was HIdIng

10

j (k)

a red BIrd Has Been dancIng
tHe taLL monster wasn't jumpIng
tHIs fat Bear wILL Be sLeepIng
our BIg dog LIkes sIngIng
tHe BaBy pIg Isn't fLyIng
your BLack cat was HIdIng

11

i

a red Bird Has Been dancing
tHe taLL monster wasn't jumping
tHIs fat Bear wiLL Be sLeeping
our Big dog Likes singing
tHe BaBy pig isn't fLying
your BLacK cat was Hiding

12

h

a red Bird has Been dancing
the taLL monster wasn't jumping
this fat Bear wiLL Be sLeeping
our Big dog Likes singing
the BaBy pig isn't fLying
your BLack cat was hiding

13

l

a red Bird has Been dancing
the tall monster wasn't jumping
this fat Bear wiLL Be sleeping
our Big dog likes singing
the BaBy pig isn't flying
your Black cat was hiding

14

b

a red bird has been dancing
the tall monster wasn't jumping
this fat bear will be sleeping
our big dog likes singing
the baby pig isn't flying
your black cat was hiding

The letter combinations **QU** and **qu** should be dealt with as they are encountered, and with the briefest of comments. This holds for the letters **X** and **Z** too.

Janice is probably reading as competently now as Eve and Jean were at the end of their sixty days. Begin teaching the following words on blocks, and as the sentence components are learned, enter them on the *X* lines of the first nine pages of the flip-flop reader. Then, as more material is learned, begin filling the *Y* lines. Finally, the *Z* lines.

1	2	3	4
policeman	which	nurse	someone
could	outside	chair	with
in	couldn't	lady	short
his	house	musn't	ceiling
car	cow	above	clown
on	must	one	standing
road	white	laughing	under
small	first	air	what
boy	shouldn't	duck	needs
floor	inside	won't	behind
doctor	teacher	hospital	tree
would	by	nice	horse
near	boat	shouting	can't
building	beside	through	two
blue	person	these	nobody
at	kitchen	windows	watching
school	thing	girl	along
farmer	between	around	brother
train		corner	over
			those

	A	B	C
page 1 X	The policeman	could be swimming	in his car.
Y	The teacher	likes skipping	by the boat.
Z	The girl	isn't eating	in the house.
page 2 X	My sister	has been jumping	on the road.
Y	The man	was singing	beside the house.
Z	A tall monster	is running	around the corner.

page 3	X	The small boy	wasn't hopping	on the floor.
	Y	That person	is dancing	in our kitchen.
	Z	Someone	will be flying	with the old pig.
page 4	X	The doctor	would be sleeping	near that building.
	Y	That black thing	likes hiding	between the houses.
	Z	The short man	isn't crying	on this ceiling.
page 5	X	A blue bird	wasn't sitting	at this school.
	Y	The nurse	was shopping	on that chair.
	Z	The fat clown	has been standing	under these windows.
page 6	X	The old farmer	should sit	in that train.
	Y	The lady	musn't sing	above the floor.
	Z	What	needs to dance	behind that tree.
page 7	X	Which frog	couldn't sit	outside the house.
	Y	Which one	is laughing	in the air.
	Z	That horse	can't swim	between the two buildings.
page 8	X	The cow	must dance	in the white house.
	Y	A small duck	won't jump	in the hospital.
	Z	Nobody	is watching	along the floor.
page 9	X	The first hen	shouldn't jump	inside this train.
	Y	That nice lady	has been shouting	through these windows.
	Z	My brother	wouldn't eat	over those houses.

ON TO BOOKS

After selecting Janice's first book, list all the new words it contains (the words your daughter has learned up to now are listed on page 203). Teach Janice the first six new words she will meet in the text, then let her read that part of the book. Continue in this way, alternating between blocks and reading. As Janice's skill improves, you will gradually be able to dispense with the blocks, and ultimately, just have her reread any sentence that contains a new word.

CHILDREN WHO WILL HAVE SPECIAL
DIFFICULTY LEARNING TO READ

In the early years, male children are often slower learners than females. In tests of the revised reading program, a four-year-old boy became so upset at the speedier progress of his three-year-old sister, his mother wisely pointed out to the children that reading was much easier for girls to do. Later, when a visitor praised the lad's reading ability, the child responded, "Yes, and it's a lot harder for a boy, too!"

But what if a child shows little progress at the end of two weeks? Have the child examined to see if he or she has a hearing impairment or faulty vision. Or, if progress is good but diminishes and stays that way when the size of type is reduced, have the child's eyes tested.

TEACHING ASSISTANTS

Some youngsters—as young as ten years of age—have a knack for charming younger children and getting them to pursue a subject. By hiring such a helper, you could give yourself an occasional break without disturbing your child's reading progress. As many as three girls ultimately taught Eve and Jean on different nights of the week, and I gladly paid double the regular baby-sitting rate.

CHOOSING BOOKS

Children's books, whether bought or borrowed, should be selected with care. Some flaws to be found in children's books are (1) too little space between lines; (2) columns too wide (narrow columns are easier to read); (3) the use of obscure words (the following words were found in elementary children's books borrowed from the library: *twinning, bade, provender, inquiringly, encircling, thrillingly, parasol*). If books are made the means of increasing a child's vocabulary, then reading becomes a chore instead of the joy it should properly be. Later, a child may indeed enlarge his or her vocabulary by reading, but vocabulary building should not be an early goal.

Authors of children's books sometimes forget that adult expressions can be puzzling for children, so we find "spend the night" used instead of "stay the night" or just plain "sleep there," "knew better than to" instead of "knew he shouldn't," and "he went on" for "he said." Avoidance of adult idioms will be especially important while your child is reading his or her first two-hundred books.

A witch in one book was described as "having a face like a bad dream," and we shouldn't be surprised if the memory of that creature upset children's sleep. Some fairy tales are peopled by grotesque characters who, if they could be projected onto the adult scale of intimidation, would make most of us sleep with a stout club handy and never climb into bed without first looking under it.

Taste in children's literature probably reaches its lowest point in the perennial favorite, *Hansel and Gretel*, wherein the stepmother and the children's natural father twice condemn the children to slow death by starvation, then a witch tries to roast them for eating. An adult movie with a plot centered on infanticide by starvation followed by attempted cannibalism might not get past the censors, and if it did, I don't think I'd want to see it.

Children have enough cares just coping with daily uncertainties and complexities without facing a clan of abominable creatures presented in the name of "pleasure" reading. The "big bad wolf" may not bother you and me, but how does he appear through the imaginative eyes of someone who hasn't yet sorted out fact from fiction? I have to admit this confusion didn't occur to me until my daughters had met big bad wolves in *Three Little Pigs* and *Goldilocks*. When I noticed the children developing a morbid fascination for the creatures, I began repeatedly pointing out that wolves of this sort lived only in books, and that real wolves try to keep away from people.

YOU'VE BAKED THE CAKE: NOW FOR THE ICING

Having taught your child to read, little more effort is required to give her a love of books. Keep your selection simple. If the books are difficult, reading becomes "that difficult pastime" in a child's mind. Make reading a privileged gift, one that is perhaps gained by doing something else well. You will know the best method for your own child. Variations of the following exchange have proven effective.

ME (*on hearing a child rummaging through a boxful of library books*): Hey, what are you doing? (*She gives me a sweet smile.*) You can't have a book just anytime you want one, you know!

DAUGHTER (*as if asking for an ice cream cone*): Can I have another book?

ME: M-m-m. Did you say "Please"?

DAUGHTER: Please?

She gets the book, and I get a warm feeling I've given her much more than a book—a present of sorts, one that won't wear out.

Eve and Jean are now readers. So is our imaginary Janice Average. Your child, however, is not imaginary, but a very real person we should now consider. Life insurance companies will provide your youngster with an endowment policy that, for a number of small monthly premiums, "endows" the child with a lump sum to pay college fees when that time arrives. This book provides your child with another sort of insurance plan—insurance that he or she will become a skillful reader and, because of it, will probably *want* to go to college. The endowment period is just sixty days. You paid, in one lump sum, all the required premiums when you purchased the book. Put the plan into operation and, quite possibly, no other two-month period in your child's life will influence the quality of it so profoundly.

MATERIALS

lined note paper
scissors
ruler
mounting putty
glue
coil-wire-bound 8½-by-11-inch exercise book
black ¼-inch felt-tip pen
black ¹/₁₆-inch felt-tip pen
red ¹/₁₆-inch felt-tip pen
6 blocks, approximately 1 inch by 2 inches by 3½ inches.
   Cut from 1-inch-by-2-inch stock, chamfer and sand to
   avoid splinters, and paint a bright color.

"blocks" playing board: Measure the distance across one
compartment in an egg container (*Fig. 50*).

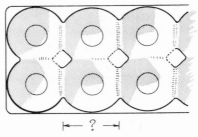

Fig. 50. An egg container.

Then mark off sixteen similar distances along an 8-by-32-inch
piece of white or colored cardboard and draw lines across
(*Fig. 51*).

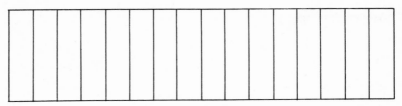

Fig. 51

Cut the egg container lengthwise down the middle, daub glue to the outside bottom of each cup, and stick the two strips at one edge of the cardboard (*Fig. 52*).

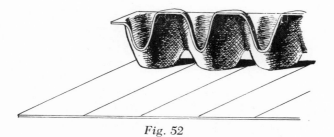

Fig. 52

The board can be made more attractive by sticking a variety of items to the lined sections—colored paper, animal pictures, decorations, and the like. Print the letters **A, B,** and **C** 1½ inches high on paper in strokes no thinner than ¼ inch. Cut around the letters and affix them to the blocks with several tiny (⅛ inch) dots of mounting putty; position the blocks as shown (*Fig. 53*). Place rewards in the cups. The child then sounds **A, B,** and **C,** moves **C** as indicated, sounds **C, A, B,** and takes the reward in the first cup. Then it is the puppet's or parent's turn to sound **C, A, B,** move the **B** over two positions, sound **B, C, A,** and take the reward in the second cup. And so on.

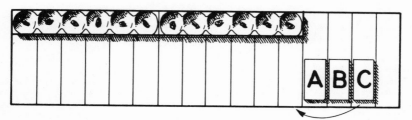

Fig. 53. "Blocks" playing board with blocks in position.

Fig. 54

Fig. 55. Positioned for the exercise.

Fig. 56. Almost anything will serve as an ambulance—even a small piece of cardboard bearing a cross.

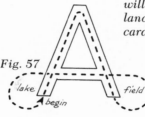

Fig. 57

An alligator named Albert was driving his ambulance along the street one day [*move the ambulance slowly up the left leg of the letter—Fig. 57*]. Suddenly [*drama*] the ambulance hit a bump. Albert heard a "snap," and when the ambulance began to steer in a strange way, Albert realized the front axle had broken. Try though he might, Albert couldn't stop the ambulance from swinging down a side street [*turn at the apex and proceed down the right leg*]. Now the brakes wouldn't work. And the ambulance went right through a dead-end street, across a field, then drove along a cross street (the crossbar), shot off the end of that street into a lake, floated around, and finally came back onto the same street where Albert had started.

By this time, the front axle was making a strange sound—**A, A, A, A**—as it drove along [*proceed over the whole route again repeating the* **A** *sound*].

Question 1. What sound does the shape tell us to make?
Question 2. What sound does the word **alligator** begin with?
Question 3. What sound does the word **Albert** begin with?
Question 4. What sound does the word **ambulance** begin with?
Question 5. What sound does the word **axle** begin with?
Question 6. What sound did the broken axle make?

A mouse named Clarence found a chocolate cookie with icing, but it was too heavy for him to carry home to his hole. Clarence didn't like the idea of eating the cookie out in the open because Cuthbert the cat was on the prowl. But Clarence was very hungry, so he began nibbling away on the cookie. Naturally, he ate the icing first. Lucky thing he did too because just then the cat appeared, and the mouse had to drop the cookie and run for his life.

Fig. 58

Question 1. What sound does the shape tell us to make?
Question 2. What sound does the name **Clarence** begin with?
Question 3. What sound does the word **cookie** begin with?
Question 4. What sound does the name **Cuthbert** begin with?
Question 5. What sound does the word **cat** begin with?
Question 6. What sound does the word **corner** begin with?

The button-nosed, bob-tailed B (sounded as for the letter **B**—see "Phonic sounds," page 165) is a shy creature who loves children; but the B is easily frightened, and usually runs away to hide behind a tree whenever boys and girls come near. So, all you may ever see of the friendly B is this:

Fig. 59

Question 1. What is the animal's name?
Question 2. What sound does **button** begin with? **Button-nosed?**
Question 3. What sound does **bob-tailed** begin with?
Question 4. See the bark on the tree. What sound does **bark** begin with?

Sammy snake liked to sleep in a curled-up position (*Fig. 60*), which resulted, unfortunately, in his frequently falling out of bed at night. In fact, Sammy fell out of bed so often that he had a scab on his back. Finally, Sammy decided to have a special bed built (*Fig. 61*), and now he doesn't fall out of bed anymore. You might like to know that snakes don't get into bed sideways—they slither in from the end. [*Trace the route of Sammy's head down to the bottom, hissing all the way.*]

Question 1. What sound does the shape tell us to make?
Question 2. What sound does the word **Sammy** begin with?
Question 3. What sound does the word **snake** begin with?
Question 4. What sound does the word **sleep** begin with?
Question 5. What sound does the word **scab** begin with?
Question 6. What sound does Sammy make as he slithers into bed?

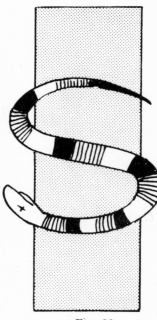

Fig. 60   Fig. 61

a
above
air
along
am
apple
around
at

baby
back
bag
be
bear
bee
been
beets
behind
beside
between
big
bird
biscuit
black
blue
boat
boy
bread
breakfast
brother
building
bus
by

cab
can
can't
car
carrot
cat
ceiling
chair
clock
clown

cob
corn
corner
could
couldn't
cow
crying
cub
cup
cut

dancing
did
dinner
do
doctor
dog
dolly
duck

eating
egg
elephant

fat
farmer
feel
feet
first
fish
floor
flying
for
frog
funny

give
green
gum

happy
has
hat
have
help

hen
hiding
his
hopping
hospital
hot
house

I
ill
in
inside
is
isn't
it

jelly
jumping

kitchen

lady
laughing
like
little
lots
lunch

man
mat
may
met
milk
monster
morning
musn't
must
my

near
neck
needs
nice
nobody
now
nurse

of
old
on
one
our
outside
over

person
pick
pig
policeman
pumpkin
puppy

red
road
running

scab
school
see
shopping
short
should
shouldn't
shouting
sick
singing
sister
sitting
skipping
sleeping
small
sock
someone
soon
standing
stew
stick
stiff
street
strong

swimming
supper

tall
tea
teacher
that
the
these
thing
this
those
through
today
train
tree
tub
two

under
up
us

want
was
wasn't
watching
we
well
what
where
which
white
who
will
windows
with
won't
would
wouldn't
wrong

you
your

Bibliography

Ames, Gillespie, and Ames, Streff. *Stop School Failure* (New York, 1972).

Arnold, Arnold. *Teaching Your Child to Learn from Birth to School Age* (Englewood Cliffs, N.J., 1971).

Ashton-Warner, Sylvia. *Teacher* (New York, 1963).

Beck, Joan. *How to Raise a Brighter Child* (New York, 1967).

Blackstone, Tessa. *A Fair Start: The Provision of Pre-School Education* (London, 1971).

Blumenfeld, Samuel L. *The New Illiterates* (New Rochelle, N.Y., 1973).

Bruner, Jerome. *The Process of Education* (New York, 1960).

Carle, Erica. "Education without Taxation." *The Freeman* (March, 1962), 48–55.

Chall, Jeanne. *Learning to Read* (New York, 1967).

Cohen, Dorothy H. *The Learning Child* (New York, 1972).

Council for Basic Education. *Phonics in Beginning Reading* (Washington, D.C., 1970).

———— *Inner City Children Can Be Taught to Read* (Washington, D.C., 1971).

Cox, Catherine. *Genetic Studies of Genius*, II (Stanford, Calif., 1926, 1959).

Daniels, Steven. *How Two Gerbils, Twenty Goldfish, Two Hundred Games, Two Thousand Books and I Taught Them How to Read* (Philadelphia, 1971).

Doman, Glenn. *How to Teach Your Baby to Read* (New York, 1963).

Durkin, Dolores. *Children Who Read Early* (New York, 1966).

———— *Teaching Young Children to Read* (Boston, 1972).

Engelmann, Siegfried. *Preventing School Failure in the Primary Grades* (New York, 1969).

Engelmann, Siegfried, and Engelmann, Therese. *Give Your Child a Superior Mind* (New York, 1966).

205

Flesch, Rudolf. *Why Johnny Can't Read* (New York, 1955).

Fuller, Renée. "Severely Retarded People Can Learn to Read." *Psychology Today* (October, 1974), 58–70.

Ginsburg, Herbert, and Opper, Silvia. *Piaget's Theory of Intellectual Development* (Englewood Cliffs, N.J., 1969).

Gordon, Julia Weber. *My Country School Diary* (New York, 1970).

Grossman, Herbert. *Nine Rotten Lousy Kids* (New York, 1972).

Harris, A. J. *How to Increase Reading Ability* (New York, 1940).

Harrison, Allan E. *How to Teach Children Twice as Much* (New York, 1973).

Her Majesty's Stationery Office. *Education: A Framework for Expansion* (London, 1972).

Holt, John. *How Children Fail* (New York, 1964).

────── *How Children Learn* (New York, 1967).

────── *The Underachieving School* (New York, 1969).

Johnson, Mary. *Programmed Illiteracy in Our Schools* (Winnipeg, 1970).

Kelley, Earl C. *Education for What Is Real* (New York, 1947).

Kirk, Samuel Alexander. "Education of the Exceptional." *Encyclopaedia Britannica*, 15th ed., *Macropaedia*, vol. 6, pp. 431–434.

Kozol, Jonathan. *Free Schools* (New York, 1972).

Lecky, Prescott. *Self-Consistency* (Hamden, Conn., 1961).

Leonard, George B. "Revolution in Education." *Look* (May 6, 1961), 58–70.

LeShan, Eda J. *The Conspiracy against Childhood* (New York, 1967).

Levy, Gerald. *Ghetto School* (New York, 1970).

Locke, John. *Some Thoughts Concerning Education* (New York, 1964).

Lorenz, Konrad Z. *King Solomon's Ring* (New York, 1962).

Love, Robert. *How to Start Your Own School* (New York, 1973).

McCracken, Glenn. *The Right to Learn* (Chicago, 1959).

McLuhan, Marshall. *The Gutenberg Galaxy* (New York, 1969).

Mill, J. S. *The Autobiography of John Stuart Mill* (New York, 1924).

Montaigne, Michel. *Of the Education of Children* (London, 1842).

Neatby, Hilda. *So Little for the Mind* (Toronto, 1949).

Neill, A. S. *Summerhill* (New York, 1960).

O'Halloran, George. *i.t.a.* (London, 1970).

Postman, Neil, and Weingartner, Charles. *Teaching as a Subversive Activity* (New York, 1969).

Pringle, M. L. Kellmer. *Able Misfits* (Atlantic Highlands, N.J., 1970).

Rafferty, Max. *Suffer, Little Children* (Old Greenwich, Conn., 1971).

Rickenbacker, William F., ed. *The Twelve Year Sentence* (La Salle, Ill., 1974).

Rosenberg, Marshall B. *Diagnostic Teaching* (Seattle, 1968).

Rousseau, Jean Jacques. *Emile* (New York, 1911).

Russell, Bertrand. *On Education* (London, 1926).

Schwebel, Milton. *Who Can Be Educated?* (New York, 1969).

Silverman, Robert E. *Psychology* (New York, 1972).

Skinner, B. F. *Walden Two* (New York, 1962).

—————— *The Technology of Teaching* (New York, 1968).

—————— *Beyond Freedom and Dignity* (New York, 1971).

Stern, Aaron. *The Making of a Genius* (Miami, 1971).

Stott, D. H. *The Parent as Teacher* (Toronto, 1972).

Terman, Lewis. *Genetic Studies of Genius*. I (Stanford, Calif., 1925, 1959).

Terman, Sybil, and Walcutt, Charles C. *Reading: Chaos and Cure* (New York, 1958).

Trace, Arther S., Jr. *What Ivan Knows that Johnny Doesn't* (New York 1961).

—————— *Reading without Dick and Jane* (Chicago, 1965).

Walcutt, Charles C. *Your Child's Reading* (New York, 1964).

—————— ed. *Tomorrow's Illiterates* (Boston, 1961).

Watson, Dorothy Taft. *Short Cuts to Reading* (Mundelein, Ill., 1965).

Wees, W. R. *Nobody Can Teach Anyone Anything* (New York, 1971).

Weiner, Norbert. *Ex-Prodigy: My Childhood and Youth* (Cambridge, Mass., 1953).

Reading Reform Foundation, 7054 East Indian School Road, Scottsdale, Arizona 85251.

Council for Basic Education, 725 Fifteenth Street N.W., Washington, D.C. 20005.